The Volga Germans

PIONEERS OF THE NORTHWEST

Areas of Volga German Settlement in the Pacific Northwest

The Volga Germans

PIONEERS OF THE NORTHWEST

Richard D. Scheuerman
and
Clifford E. Trafzer

University Press of Idaho

ISBN 0-89301-073-1
Library of Congress Card number 80-52314
Copyright © 1985 by the University Press of Idaho
Manufactured in the United States of America
Cover design by Debra Moloshok

Published by the University Press of Idaho — A Division of the Idaho Research Foundation, Inc. Box 3368, University Station, Moscow, Idaho 83843

Cover Photograph : C.J. Lust Family, from the photographs of R.A. Hutchison, Washington State University Libraries, Pullman, Wash.

8- 7- 86

To all those who so willingly shared with us their stories
And to five remarkable aunts:
Lena, Mildred, Margaret, Evelyn, and Lorraine

PREFACE

This story deals with one of the largest migrations by a single ethnic group to the Pacific Northwest. It is the saga of the Volga Germans who settled in this region and has a scenario stretching from Germany and Russia. It explores their European origins in the eighteenth century and investigates the remarkable program of colonization inaugurated in the 1760s under the Russian empress, Catherine II. The revocation of the original terms of settlement by the Russian Senate in 1871 resulted in the immigration to North America of over 100,000 Volga Germans. They joined other immigrant waves to the New World in transforming the United States and Canada into centers of Western productivity while influencing North American religion, politics and social development.

The Volga Germans first settled in the Midwest but with the advent of railroads to the Pacific Northwest in the early 1880s, a significant number began moving to that region. Their involvement in the westward movement provides a valuable case study of the techniques involved in the settlement campaigns undertaken by the northwest railroads, principally Henry Villard's Northern Pacific. It is also illustrative of the interaction between ethnicity and geography in determining regional settlement patterns.

Without the assistance of many helpful people, this narrative could not have been completed. We are deeply indebted to Dr. Phillip Nordquist of Pacific Lutheran University in Tacoma, Washington for his advice concerning the organization and writing of this work. His many helpful suggestions involving aspects of European history and his encouragement have been greatly appreciated. We are equally grateful to Dr. Emmett Eklund for his most enlightening remarks on religious history and his abiding interest in this project. The guidance of Dr. Arthur Martinson and the late Dr. Herman Deutsch in matters relating to Northwest history is gratefully acknowledged. We would also like to thank Donald Messerschmidt, David Stratton, William Willard,

5

and Thomas Kennedy of Washington State University who have supported our research endeavors.

Several noted authors on the subject of Volga German history have rendered great service by providing relevant materials, notably Mrs. Emma S. Haynes, Arlington, Virginia and Mr. Fred Koch, Olympia, Washington. Mrs. Haynes' untiring devotion to this project resulted in the documentation through passenger ship manifests of virtually every family in the original Kansas and Nebraska colonies which immigrated to the Pacific Northwest between 1881 and 1882. Our sincere gratitude is expressed to Dr. Karl Stumpp, Tübingen, West Germany, the eminent authority on the Germans from Russia, for his encouragement and permission to use his excellent series of maps. Glen Adams, whose name is synonymous with Northwest Americana publishing, and Professor Earl Larrison at the University Press of Idaho (Moscow) deserve thanks for supporting Russian German studies and bringing them into public view. We also thank the many western chapters of the American Historical Society of Germans from Russia (AHSGR) for providing both photographs to illustrate this work and a forum in which to conduct many hours of oral interviews.

No work of this nature could ever have been possible without the co-operation of capable local historians through whom we were led to valuable contacts, new information and warm friendships. We thank Mr. and Mrs. Roy Oestreich of Ritzville; Mr. and Mrs. Alvin Kissler (Seattle), formerly from Odessa; Miss Jean Roth (Seattle) and Mrs. Elaine Davison for their help on the Walla Walla settlement; Mrs. Anna Weitz, Endicott; Mr. and Mrs. Ray Reich, Colfax; and Alec Horst, Tacoma. Mr. Fred Kromm of Spokane, Mr. William Scheirman of Overland Park, Kansas, and Mrs. Leon Scheuerman of Deerfield, Kansas, also provided valuable source materials. Information gleaned through interviewing first generation immigrants formed a vast reserve of detail essential to this study, participants are listed in the Bibliography. Informants of special note include Mrs. Catherine Luft, Sheboygan, Wisconsin; Mr. Martin Lust, Walla Walla; Mr. Conrad Blumenschein, St. John; Mr. Dave

Schierman, College Place; Mr. C.G. Schmick, Colfax; and the late Mr. Alec Reich and Mr. Karl Scheuerman, both of Endicott. In addition, a number of pastors and their families have willingly co-operated and permitted access to most useful sources of information. Appreciation is extended to the Rev. H. Reike family, Rev. K.A. Horn family, Rev. Albert Hausauer, and other pastors and laymen involved in this study.

Staff services at several institutions were greatly appreciated, particularly at Pacific Lutheran University by Mr. Richard Grefrath and Mrs. Helen Leraas, librarians, Mortvedt Library; Esther Fromm at the Archives of the American Historical Society of Germans from Russia in Greeley, Colorado; John Guido and Terry Abraham, archivists, Holland Library, Washington State University; Rev. Robert C. Wiederaenders, Church Archivist, the American Lutheran Church Archives, Dubuque, Iowa and its North Pacific District Archive in Seattle. Thankfulness is also extended to Mrs. Henny Hysky, curator, the Vogelsberg Museum in Schotten, West Germany for her co-operation and assistance and to Mrs. Bob Griffith of Cashmere, and Wayne Rosenoff of Monterey for their encouragement.

Several individuals generously shared their expertise in translating letters and other rare materials; we thank Mrs. Selma Muller, Tacoma; Mrs. Hilda Weirich, Dryden; and Miss Marite Sapiets of the Institute for the Study of Religion and Communism in London. Unless otherwise indicated, the chapter epigraphs were translated by Mrs. Muller from Volga German folk songs included in Erbes' and Sinner's, *Volkslieder und Kinderreime aus den Wolgakolonien* (1914). Invaluable assistance in the preparation of this manuscript was given by Lois Scheuerman and Cindy DeGrosse and the encouragement extended by our parents is also gratefully acknowledged.

Note

A variety of names for the Germans from Russia are commonly used in historical sources dealing with the subject. In the course of this study, the term "Russian German" is used in a collective sense as a German from any part of Russia.

The term "Volga Germans" indicates only those Germans who lived along the lower Volga River and similarly qualified terms (e.g., Black Sea Germans) refer to Germans of specific geographical origin in Russia. Until 1918 the Julian Calendar was still used in Russia. By the twentieth century it had fallen thirteen days behind the Gregorian Calendar of the Western World, losing one day per century between 1700 and 1900. Dates registered in Russian sources during that time reflect the Old Style system (O.S.) and will be used in reference to that period throughout this study unless indicated otherwise by the initials N.S. (New Style). When both German and Russian terms appear following their translation in the text, they will be indicated in sequence as follows: (Russian/German).

Abbreviations used in footnoting books and serial publications include the following (complete documentation for each is provided in the Bibliography):

DWD—Krause and others, *Denkschrift zum Silber-Jubiläum des Washington Distrikts der Ev. Luth. Ohio Synode, 1891-1916.*

VRS—Schwabenland, *A History of the Volga Relief Society.*

LS—*Lutheran Standard.*

AHSGR—American Historical Society of Germans from Russia.

Richard D. Scheuerman
Clifford E. Trafzer
Pullman, Washington
April 22, 1980

CONTENTS

ILLUSTRATIONS

11

12

MAPS

TABLES

FOREWORD

The term "Volga German" often leaves Americans baffled, and the comment is sometimes made, "How can these people be Germans when their ancestors came from Russia?" Richard Scheuerman and Clifford Trafzer answer this question by explaining the colonization campaign undertaken by Catherine the Great in which western Europeans were invited to settle in Russia. About 27,000 people, primarily from Hesse and the Palatinate, founded 104 colonies on both banks of the Volga near the city of Saratov in the 1760s. In spite of many difficulties, they soon succeeded in bringing this area under cultivation.

After a century had passed, many of the settlement privileges which had been granted by Catherine were rescinded. The most important of these was freedom from military service. Beginning with the year 1874, Germans were expected to serve in the Russian army. This, coupled with poor economic conditions, resulted in an exodus to the New World.

The authors relate the experiences of two brothers, Johann Adam and Matthais Repp, who journeyed from the Volga to America in the 1850s and acquired land southeast of Humboldt, Kansas. However, at the outbreak of the Civil War they returned to Russia. During the following decade when Volga German emigration from Russia surged, Johann Adam Repp joined a large group of his people and came back to Kansas in 1876. Many of these immigrants were Lutheran and pietistic "brethren," some of whom joined such churches in America as the Congregational, Baptist, Mennonite and Seventh-Day Adventist.

However, the attention of the authors focuses particularly on the dramatic story of Volga German immigration to the Pacific Northwest. This was begun primarily from two areas of Volga German settlement in the Midwest — Kansas and Nebraska. Life in Kansas was very difficult during these early years and Volga Germans there formed a nucleus from which Russian German immigration to the Pacific Northwest was

14

begun in 1881. Having heard from railroad workers that the climate in Oregon was mild and that fertile land was available, they decided to leave for the Pacific coast. In 1881 they traveled to San Francisco over the Union Pacific's transcontinental line and then went on to Portland by steamship. At first they worked at temporary jobs, but many longed to have farms of their own and soon a scouting expedition was sent to view lands in the Palouse country of Washington which were for sale through Henry Villard's Oregon Improvement Company. The scouts returned favorably impressed and in the fall of 1882 most members of the Portland group left for Whitman County by covered wagon and steamship.

Volga Germans from the colonies of Kolb and Dietel had arrived in Nebraska in August 1876. Many members of this group acquired land in Culbertson where they were joined two years later by other Volga Germans from Kolb and Frank, Russia. A segment of this group also decided to immigrate westward and early in 1882 a number of families boarded a train at North Platte, Nebraska for Ogden, Utah. Here they formed a train of forty wagons with which they followed the Oregon Trail to Walla Walla, Washington. They arrived in the summer of 1882 and most decided to winter there although several families continued on to Portland. Some of the Volga Germans chose to settle in Walla Walla while others continued on and established prosperous farmsteads in Adams, Lincoln and Klickitat Counties. From these outposts Volga German settlement expanded throughout the Columbia Basin, on the coast and into northern Idaho, British Columbia and Alberta.

Central to the story is the religious life of the Volga Germans. Their participation in the growth of the various Lutheran synods is portrayed as is the role of the German Congregational Church and pioneer missionaries. A review is given of the Volga Relief Society which was organized in Portland, Oregon and which raised money throughout the United States for German famine sufferers in Russia from 1921 to 1923.

This is a book which is well worth reading, not only by all

Volga Germans of the Pacific Northwest but by those in other states as well. It presents a notable chapter in the history of the Germans from Russia.

Emma S. Haynes
Washington, D.C.
July 31, 1980

INTRODUCTION

In the German village of Nidda in the state of Hesse stands a small stone structure with a single entrance, its massive wooden door crowned by a plaque on which is inscribed: *Der Johanniterturm: Ältestes und ehrwürdigstes Baudenkmal der Stadt...Im 30 jährigen Krieg zerstört.* Built during Medieval times, it was once part of the palatial residence of a prominent family but since its destruction in the Thirty Years War (1618-48), it stands alone in the town as a silent reminder of an earlier time in German history when wars ravaged the region. It was from such villages in Hesse and Rhine Palatinate that thousands of people came in the 1760s to seek a new life elsewhere and while many during this period migrated to the American colonies, others looked eastward to Russia.

There were several factors that led to this movement, many of which were a culmination of events that began with the Reformation. Martin Luther's remarks in 1521 at the Diet of Worms essentially questioned the authority of the Roman Catholic Church but thousands of peasants perceived the spirit of reform and Luther's concern for Christian liberty as challenging the very foundations of the oppressive feudal system. German princes and nobles realized the political implications of Luther's theology and sought to assert their political ambitions by breaking away from the control of the Holy Roman Empire. In short, the Reformation advanced a three-fold revolution involving religious, social, and political upheaval.

Early Lutheran converts in the German nobility included Phillip of Hesse, Ulrich of Württemburg, John of Saxony, and others.[1] The German Diet soon became hopelessly divided over religious issues which continued to be debated while popular discontent seethed in the countryside. Sporadic peasant revolts against ecclesiastical and secular authorities occurred from 1522 to 1524, erupting in the ruinous Peasants War (1524-26).

In 1526 the landgrave of Hesse, Phillip the Magnanimous,

formed the League of Gothe and Torgau with John the Steadfast of Saxony in order to solidify and extend Lutheranism and within two years the Lutheran Church had been established in half of Germany. This did not prevent internal struggles, however, as later in the sixteenth century Lutherans and Calvinists often alternated roles in princely capacities, expelling one another from positions of authority while expecting a corresponding change in the theology of the citizenry. Protestants did unite in the last great religious war in Europe, arising out of a dispute with the Hapsburgs in 1618 over a successor to the Bohemian throne. Over the decades of fighting in the Thirty Years War, no region suffered as much as Hesse and the Rhine Palatinate.[2] Due to their strategic location between the opposing forces of the southern Catholic states and the Protestants in the north with their ally France, the area was recurrently ravaged by invading armies. Though the German princes eventually asserted themselves over the Catholic Hapsburgs, the cost in human suffering was horrendous.[3]

Recovery after the Treaty of Westphalia (1648) was further compounded in Hesse-Cassel and Hesse-Darmstadt as the two states became embroiled in a fratricidal war, the *Hessenkrieg*.[4] Foreign expansion into the area was renewed by the French under Louis XIV in 1688 when he dispatched troops to the Rhine after the League of Augsburg refused to accept his claim to a portion of the Elector Palantine's estate. The aggressive policies of the French king led to a full scale invasion of the Rhineland resulting in disastrous conflagrations in the major cities along the Rhine from Phillipsburg to Bingen.

In the struggles which ensued, the French laid waste to large areas of southeast Germany and although hostilities in the War of the Palatinate (1689-97) were suspended through the Peace of Ryswick, French designs on the area contributed to renewed outbreaks of fighting in the Wars of Spanish Succession (1701-13) and Austrian Succession (1740-48). Each successive campaign exposed a new generation to the ravages of warfare, and while the peasantry bore the cruel consequences, their rulers soon made arrangements to profit from

18

the situation.

Hesse-Cassel in particular provided thousands of mercenaries at foreign expense to fight in Europe during the Seven Years War (1756-63). Although the two Hessian states were again divided by political alliances, the leadership of both houses was characterized by corruption and extravagance, notably Hesse-Darmstadt under Ludwig VII and Ludwig VIII. Whenever burdensome taxes could not support the opulent life of the baroque court, the selling of mercenaries to foreign powers became a convenient method of raising the needed revenue.[5]

The Seven Years War had a major impact on emigration from Germany to Russia for two principal reasons. Hesse again became the scene of great decimation throughout the conflict and, secondly, this period witnessed the acension of Catherine II, a former German princess, to the Romanov throne in Russia. Prussian advances against the French had been challenged in Hesse by the Duc de Broglie in the spring of 1759 when French forces repulsed the Prussians under Ferdinand of Brunswick northwest of Frankfurt a.M. at Bergen. These gains were reversed however when on August 1, 1759 Ferdinand routed the French in a decisive victory at Minden. The retreating French soldiers wreaked havoc on the German countryside, destroying crops and ransacking villages.

Russia entered the conflict under Tsarina Elisabeth, allied with France and Austria against the Prussians and English. Despite heavy losses on all sides, the war continued for years until the balance of power unexpectedly shifted with the Tsarina's death in January, 1762 (N.S.). At her request a nephew then assumed power, the feeble-minded Peter III, who immediately reversed the Russian position into an alliance with Frederick II of Prussia whom he admired as the ideal monarch.[6]

The stuggles continued into the next decade, exacting a catastrophic loss of human life, and the assistance rendered Frederick by Russia in 1762 was short-lived as a *coup d' etat* on June 28 in St. Petersburg established Catherine II as "Empress and Autocrat of all the Russians." Her husband, Peter III, was killed days later under circumstances never officially explained. Catherine ordered her generals out of the war. Battle-scarred Europe was exhausted and ready for peace but the settlements reached in 1763 did little to ease the plight of the peasants. Prussian hegemony would become increasingly evident in northern Europe although near the end of the eighteenth century Germany seemed hopelessly divided into over 1700 states, principalities, and free cities. The Hessian states were bankrupt and resorted to a program of heavy taxation while returning soldiers formed marauding bands which terrorized the populace.[7] A report from Hesse-Darmstadt dated April 4, 1767 reported:

> The excessive burden of debt and the poverty prevailing at present among the prince's subjects originating partly in the last destructive war, partly in the cattle epidemic existing in many places, partly in the disastrous fluctuating of money values, the creditless and impoverished conditions of the royal subjects; and in addition to this, the present low price of grain, all taken together make the poor subjects unable to pay their present debts or to save themselves from those previously made.[8]

Local magistrates suggested various schemes through which taxes could be reduced, problems between creditors and debtors ameliorated, public granaries established, and various other programs which could alleviate the tragic situation of the peasantry. Unfortunately the princes only listened, taking little action as the masses wasted away in misery or wandered off in attempts to create a new life.[9] Fully a half-dozen generations in such areas of Germany had experienced the deprivation and atrocities of European wars and while many remained, others prepared to emigrate.[10]

In *Briefe über die Auswanderung der Unterhanen besonders nach Russland* (Gotha, 1770), twenty letters appear dealing with the emigration and one by a Herr von Loen reveals the pitiful conditions of the German peasants while blaming the princes themselves for causing their subjects to flee.

> In our time the farmer is the unhappiest of beings; the peasants are slaves; and their labor we can scarcely distinguish from that of the animals which they herd. If you visit a village, you will see children running about half-naked, loudly begging you for alms; their parents have only a few rags to cover their nakedness; two or three scrawny cows must plow the fields and furnish them milk; their granaries are empty; their huts are on the verge of collaps-

20

ing, and they themselves present a most pitiful appearance.

Woe to those princes who by their lusts, tyranny, and mismanagement bring misfortune on so many people! The peasant is always threatened with feudal serfdom, pressed service as messengers, hunting service and digging fortifications. From morning to night he must work the fields over and over, whether the sun remains in the fields, almost becoming a wild beast himself in order to frighten off wild beasts so they do not destroy the crops. That which he saves from the wild beasts is taken by the cruel officers for arrears of taxes.

...What is he to do? The most justifiable course consistent with his duty is to leave the land which is unworthy of good citizens and seek another where such citizens are valued and sought after. So he leaves, though willingly, his homeland, his acquaintances and friends, the social life he enjoys, and so on. With a sorrowful heart, he chooses, as a wise man, the lesser of two evils; he prefers to risk his fortunes rather than remain in a country where his ruin is inevitable.[11]

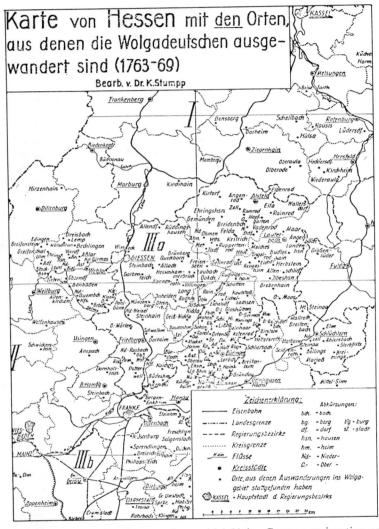

Map 1. Hesse, showing the areas from which Volga German emigration occurred (1763-69)

1
THE PROGRAM OF IMMIGRATION UNDER CATHERINE II

Das Manifest der Kaiserin,
Es dachte nach den Deutschen
hin,
Sie sollten pflanzen Brot und
Wein,
Und sollten auch Kolonisten
sein.

The Empress Catherine's Manifest,
It thought the Germans would be
best.
They were to raise both wine and
bread,
And also be colonists, it said.

—"Das Manifest," v. 1

Shortly after the close of the Seven Years War, Catherine II of Russia (1762-96) issued on July 22, 1763 the Manifesto of the Empress that succeeded in luring thousands of Germans to the vast southwest frontier of her empire. This was actually the result of a program originated by Tsarina Elisabeth Petrovna (1741-62) who as early as 1752 had considered peopling the Turkish border region with French Protestants at the suggestion of a French immigration official, de la Fonte.[1] A committee was appointed to consider the project and an active program was formulated only to be tabled when the Seven Years War broke out in Europe, without any French being settled in the area.

The idea was perpetuated and given new vigor after Catherine II was crowned tsarina as she had long held grandiose plans for modernizing Russia. Even as a grand duchess married to the heir to the throne, she wrote "We need people. We must make our wide spaces teem with swarms of people if

23

this be possible."[2] Peter the Great (1689-1725), a century earlier, had launched an ambitious campaign to modernize his backward nation, as Russia in the eighteenth century was just emerging from a quasi-Medieval existence due to centuries of cultural isolation from Europe. The Petrine reforms succeeded in instituting limited technological and social change by opening the door to Western thought and culture. Under his reign, the capitol was moved from Moscow to St. Petersburg, Russia's new port on the Baltic and Peter's "Window to the West." In addition Peter induced over 1,000 German officers and engineers to come to Russia in order to expand trade relations with Europe, construct this new capitol, and reshape the government bureaucracy.[3] The influx of Germans under his reign led in 1703 to the construction of a wooden Lutheran church in St. Petersburg. These and other German immigrations into Russia up until 1750 largely constituted what Karl Stumpp has termed the "Urban German element" solicited by the crown from 1550 to 1750.[4]

Another policy initiated by Peter and perpetuated by his successors, that would later be associated with German migrations to Russia, was the calculated intermarriage of the Romanov family with German princely houses. In the case of Peter the Great, his son Alexis married the princess of Brunswick-Wolfenbüttel in 1711 and in 1725 his daughter Anne married the Duke of Holstein.[5] The result was such that the Russian royal family was almost entirely German by blood at the time Catherine II became tsarina in 1762.

Catherine II was born in Stettin, Germany, in 1729, the daughter of the Prince of Anhalt-Zerbst, a minor principality in Saxony. Named Sophie Auguste Fredericka, she was brought to St. Petersburg at the age of 16 by Empress Elisabeth Petrovna to marry the heir apparent to the throne, later Peter III. Following the palace revolt which unseated him in 1762, Catherine capably assumed the responsibilities as head of state and began to implement plans to reform her backward country in the spirit of Peter the Great. On ascending the throne Catherine declared that her chief task would be "to devote care and attention to the peace and prosperity of the Empire's wide expanses of territory, which

God had entrusted to her, and to the increase of its inhabitants."[6] An intelligent and clever woman, she mastered the Russian language and became devoted to Russia's growth and prosperity. A key element of her program involved the colonization of the fertile lower Volga region which for centuries had stood idle near the unstable Turkish border, virtually, "a happy hunting ground for adventurers, vagrants, bands of marauders and river pirates."[7] Both the eastern plains side (*Wiesenseite*) of the lower Volga and the hilly western side (*Bergseite*) were inhabited by a variety of nomadic peoples of Turkic and Mongolian descent including the Tatars, Bashkirs, Kirghiz, and Kalmyks.[8]

Since a prerequisite to the continuation of her ambitious policies was the cooperation of the Russian aristocracy, Catherine found it both unwise and impractical to suggest that the institution of serfdom be altered in order to provide the Russian peasantry with the opportunity to colonize the frontiers. While not only challenging the order of the nobility on whose support she depended, Catherine realized that the peasants themselves were incapable of effective colonization. Writing to the new commission investigating the subject Catherine wrote:

> Russia not only does not have enough inhabitants but it also has such vast expanses of land which are neither populated or cultivated. So enough incentive cannot be found for the state population to increase... To restore an Empire, denuded of inhabitants, it is useless to expect help from the children who in the future may be born. Such a hope is in any case untimely; people living in these open spaces of theirs have no zeal or incentive. Fields which could feed a whole people hardly provide enough food for one household....[9]

The logical solution to the dilemma was to summon capable foreign colonists to Russia in order that they "might by their acquired arts, handicrafts, industry, and various machinery as yet unknown in Russia, reveal to Russian citizens the easiest and most efficient ways of tilling the ground, breeding domestic animals, nurturing forests, making the fullest use of all products, establishing their own factories, and regulating the entire peasant economy."[10] This philosophy was a part of the eighteenth century. Central to

25

this concept was that agriculture was the basic form of productive labor, and that only through its ties to trade and industry could the national wealth increase.[11] This policy was in contrast to mercantilistic conceptions of economic growth dominant in Western Europe and pursued previously by the Empress Elisabeth who sought to extend the financial base of the economy by employing new methods of manufacturing, principally through the silk and fur industries.

However, Catherine did in part resurrect the framework of Elisabeth's earlier scheme to bring French Protestants into Russia as she was particularly impressed with the manner in which the French farmers had transformed the "marshy, sandy, and infertile domains of the King of Prussia" into a region of great productivity.[12] In a decree written personally by the empress and delivered to the Russian Senate on October 14, 1762, Catherine ordered immediate cooperation with the Foreign Office to facilitate the entry of all foreigners, wishing to enter Russia.[13] Her manifesto of December 4, 1762 gave the program further impetus and more active measures were taken to inform European peoples of settlement opportunities in Russia as the senate was ordered to publish the manifest "in all languages and in all foreign newspapers."[14] A decree on December 29 directed the Russian Foreign Office to distribute hundreds of copies of the manifesto in various languages to their diplomatic representatives. Furthermore, the Russian ambassadors and representatives were ordered to "not only make known the Manifesto by publishing it in the usual trade periodicals, but also to make every effort to see that it has an effect."[15]

The appeal brought little response. The conflict on the continent brought on by the Seven Years War had still not been resolved and the general feeling of the Russian diplomats was that Catherine's pledge of "imperial kindness and benevolence"[16] in the Manifesto was hardly sufficient to attract a significant number of colonists. Writing from London to his uncle the Russian chancellor, Count Vorontsov stated that, "A mere promise to accept those who apply will not attract a large number of settlers, for in that case they will be leaving a situation where they have some hope of security in order to enter a completely unknown situation."[17]

After considering these observations, the Foreign Office submitted a report to the senate recommending payment for each settler's travel expenses since it was assumed it was largely the poor who desired to emigrate and asked for clarification of such issues as which areas would be open to foreign colonist settlement, what benefits and facilities would be available to them and how their transport would be arranged once in Russia. In addition the Senate was reminded of Elisabeth's earlier scheme negotiated with de la Fonte and these proposals were attached in order to help resolve the question.

The program may well have succumbed to the same fate as other long pending legislation in the bureaucratic committee of the senate had not Catherine personally intervened in the matter. At her insistence, a list of privileges and conditions were drafted under the supervision of the procurator-general, A. I. Glebov, to form the July 22, 1763 Manifesto of the Empress Catherine II.[18] As the foundation of Russia's new colonization policy, it became the instrument through which thousands of impoverished Europeans, primarily Germans, were enabled to begin a new life in Russia between 1763 and 1766.[19]

Variously termed a "masterpiece of immigration propaganda" and the "Magna Carta"[20] of the German colonists in Russia, the manifesto enumerated the conditions of settlement summarized as follows:[21]

1. All foreigners received permission to settle in any Russian province by declaring their desire to do so to the Chancery for the Guardianship of Foreigners (*Tutel-Kanzlei für Ausländer/Kantselyariya Opekunstra Inostrantsev*) in St. Petersburg or to the proper authorities of Russian border towns. Prospective colonists who lacked the means to settle elsewhere need only to apply to the Russian diplomatic representative who would, at the expense of the crown, supply them with the money for travel expenses.

2. On arrival in Russia the settlers had to declare whether they wanted to register as merchants, industrialists, or if they desired to form farming settlements in appropriate areas. In

accordance with their response they received assignments after taking the oath of allegiance in accordance with their faith.

3. In addition other rights and privileges were granted:

a) Freedom of religion was guaranteed with the right to construct churches and belfries and to maintain pastors and other church officials. Proselyting Christians of other faiths in Russia was strictly forbidden although converting Moslems was permitted.

b) The colonists were to be immune from all taxes, military, and government service; both "ordinary and extraordinary" for those who settled in colonies in uninhabited territories, this to last thirty years after which they would be under the same obligation as native Russians to pay taxes and carry out local government service. However, they were freed "for eternal time" from military service.

c) Settlers were to receive sufficient land well-suited to growing grain as well as for building factories and other new industries for which special subsidies and exemption would be allowed.

d) Foreign industrialists who built factories in Russia at their own expense could purchase the necessary serfs and peasants.

e) Ten-year interest-free loans were given for building, to obtain livestock, and agricultural implements.

f) Permission was granted to import specified amounts of personal property and settlers were guaranteed freedom to return to their countries of origin, though a portion of their property would be relinquished to the state.

g) Colonists had the right of local self-government within the limits of Russian state law.

h) Settlers were allowed to organize duty-free markets and fairs in the colonies they established.

i) Upon arrival in Russia, settlers were allotted money for their sustenance and transport to the assigned areas of settlement.

j) The final section of the manifesto allowed any settler wishing to discuss other privileges to address his request to the government.

Fig. 1. Büdingen, Germany in the seventeenth century. (The Frankfurt am Main Historical Museum)

29

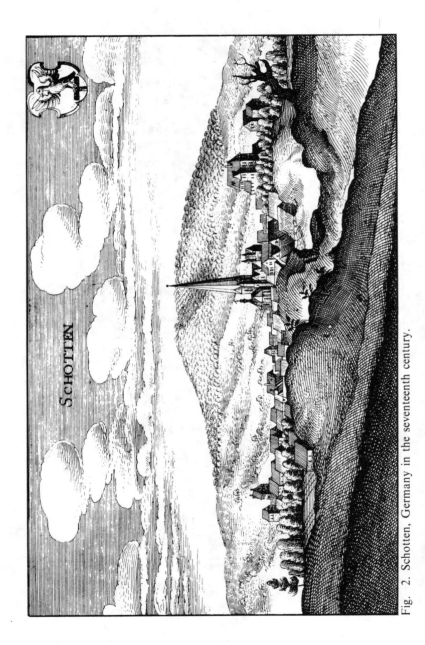

Fig. 2. Schotten, Germany in the seventeenth century.

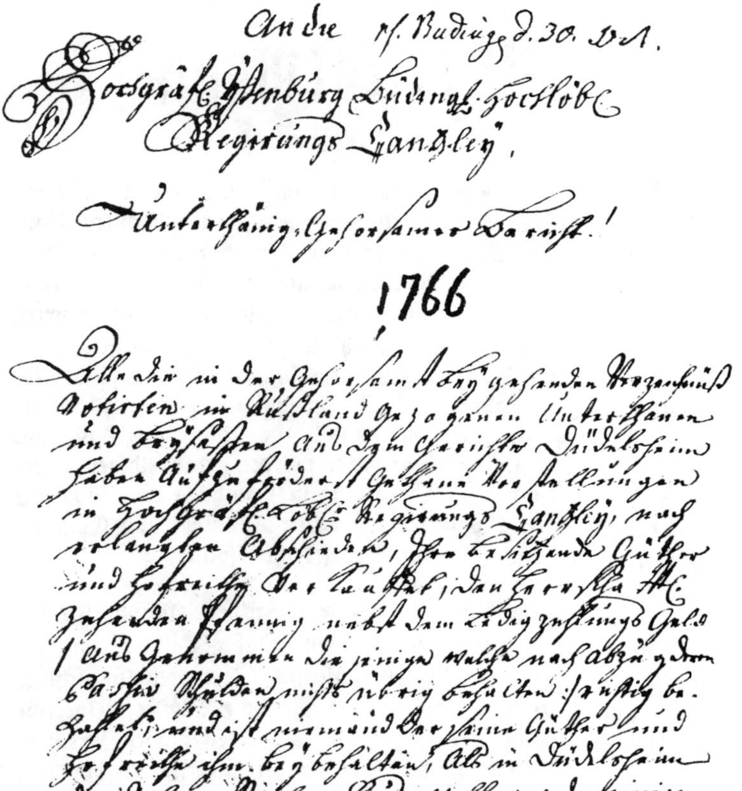

An die … Büdingen d. 30. Oct.
Hochgräfl. Ysenburg Büdingische Hochlöbl.
Regierungs Canzley.

Unterthänig gehorsamer Bericht!

1766

Fig. 3. Isenburg-Büdingen court report on emigration to Russia, 1766. (Mrs. Emma S. Haynes and the Büdingen Castle Library)

Avertiſſement.

Nachdem es ohnehin ſchon offenkündig iſt, daß alle und jede Ausländer, welche ſich vermöge des allerhöchſten Ruſ-ſiſch Kaiſerlichen Manifeſts de dato Peterhof den 22ſten Julii 1763. in dem Ruſſiſchen Reiche häuslich niederlaſſen, und inſon-derheit bey dem Anbau fruchtbarer, aber noch uncultivirten Ländereyen, eine gute und reichliche Nahrung ſuchen wollen, von den Ruſſiſch Kayſerlichen Geſandtſchaften durchgängig die willfährigſte Aufnahme und Förderung zu gewarten haben: So dienet hiermit weiter männiglich zur Nachricht, daß nun-mehro auch die Anſtalt iſt getroffen worden, daß ſelbigen ſofort nach ihrer Ankunft und Anmeldung in Hamburg oder in Lübeck bey den dortigen Ruſſiſch Kaiſerlichen Miniſtris und Commiſ-ſarius, nachſtehende Vortheile angedeihen ſollen:

Erſtens empfängt täglich eine erwachſene Manns-Perſon Acht Schilling, eine Weibs-Perſon Fünf Schilling, und ein Kind, ohne Unterſchied des Geſchlechts, Drey Schilling ſchwer Geld zum Unterhalt, welches in Reichs-Münze reſpective ohngefehr zwanzig Kreuzer, zwölf und einen halben Kreuzer, dann ſieben und einen halben Kreuzer beträgt, mithin für eine ganze Familie etwas nahmhaftes ausmachet.

Zweytens wird in Hamburg für ihre gemächliche und wohlfeile Einquartierung, bis zur Zeit ihrer Abreiſe nach Lü-beck, Sorge getragen, und allenfalls noch, zur Erleichterung der kurzen Reiſe von Hamburg nach Lübeck, für die Weiber und kleinen Kinder ein Fuhrwerk verſchaffet.

Fig. 4. Leaflets such as these were distributed throughout Germany en-couraging people to emigrate to Russia. (Dr. Karl Stumpp)

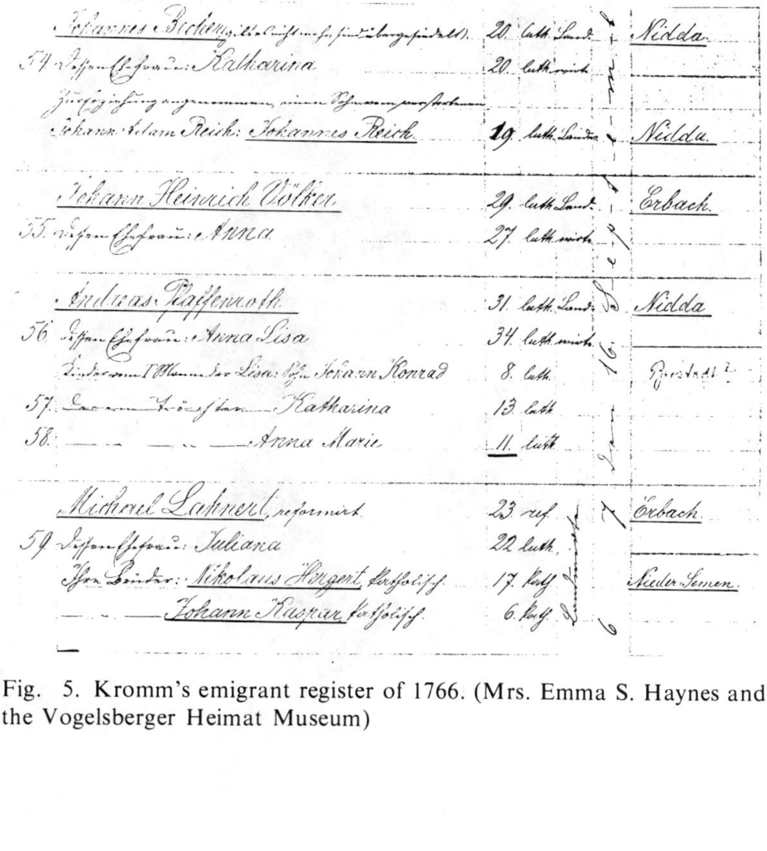

Fig. 5. Kromm's emigrant register of 1766. (Mrs. Emma S. Haynes and the Vogelsberger Heimat Museum)

Fig. 6. Empress Catherine II, by F. S. Rokotov, 1779.

Fig. 7. Gregory Orlov, by F. S. Rokotov.

Section II of an attached register of vacant lands specified a vast area up and down the Volga River from Saratov in the province of Astrakhan. It was to this region in particular that the colonists were directed.

In July of 1763, on the same day that the manifesto was promulgated, a second decree established a special government department to administer the anticipated flood of foreign settlement. The Chancery for the Guardianship of Foreigners was responsible only to the empress and given far-reaching authority. As the equivalent of a government ministry, its central functions were to supervise the Russian representatives of the program throughout Europe and arrange for colonist transportation and payments. Headed by the appointed president who was a person favorite of the empress, Count Gregory Orlov supervised operations in what was destined to become a ponderous bureaucracy which often led to disastrous incidents during settlement.[22] With an enormous annual budget of 200,000 rubles, the *Tutel-Kanzlei* consisted of several counselors appointed by the president, a "special secretary with a knowledge of foreign languages" to adjudicate diplomatic problems, lesser bureaucrats, translators[23] and, later, immigrant agents in Europe.

Despite the favorable intentions of the Russian diplomats in Europe, it became increasingly difficult to execute their normal responsibilities while directing immigration activities and in 1764 only about 400 families arrived in Russia,[24] most from Westphalia with others from Scandinavia. Mismanagement was widespread as scores of disreputable individuals received financial support initially, only to refuse to emigrate at the appointed time.[25] It also became evident that opposition to the program was widespread throughout Europe and only in England, Holland, and southwestern Germany did the activities of the recruiting agents initially meet little opposition. These areas of Germany were particularly receptive to Catherine's invitation, due to the religious conflicts, abject poverty caused by the wars, and the corrupt rule of the princes. Centers for departure to Russia during this early state were established in Regensburg, Freiburg, Roslau, Worms, and elsewhere.

Due to the great response in the two Hessian states of Cassel and Darmstadt and in the Rhineland, it was decided to concentrate a major effort of the colonization campaign there under the authority of the Russian ambassador to the Reichstag at Regensburg, Johann Simolin. In an effort to alleviate the deceptive practices of some prospective emigrants, the program underwent two important revisions in Germany at Simolin's recommendation. Since previous experience demonstrated the difficulties of transportation and regular payment of expenses during overland treks to Russia, the procedure was systematized by selecting Lübeck in December, 1763, as the central gathering and dispersal point to Russia. A reliable merchant there, Heinrich Schmidt, was appointed special commissioner in May, 1764 to supervise the operations.[26] From there Hanseatic or English vessels shipped the emigrants to Kronstadt near St. Petersburg.[27]

The *Tutel-Kanzlei* also found it advisable to offer proprietorships to individuals capable of organizing scores of emigrants for settlement in Russia. Several French immigration recruiters responded, most of whom acted with numerous independent agents through unscrupulous tactics to entice people to emigrate.[28] The fraudulent methods they utilized to fill various transport quotas led to their designation in such terms as *Menschenfänger* (people catchers) and *Seelenverkäufer* (soul sellers).[29] While they succeeded in attracting thousands to Russia, their approach was condemned by Simolin whose more orderly program involved, as much as possible, the sanction of local authorities.[30] As the combined effect of these efforts grew, particularly in Germany, the ruling families realized that their labor force and tax base was steadily eroding and responded with legislation restricting emigration. In 1764 action was taken in the German states of Bavaria, Saxony, Hamburg, and Würzburg to forbid further emigration to Russia and in the following year Frederick II of Prussia followed by taking steps to remove the foreign agents from his county.[31]

By 1766 it had become clear to Simolin and the various French recruiters that concentrated work in areas of southern Germany where the ruinous effects of the Seven Years War were still widespread would be advantageous. Simolin was assisted in his endeavors by two German special commissioners, Friedrich Meixner in Ulm and Johann Facius, headquartered in Frankfurt a.M., beneath whom functioned a number of German agents at various assembly points. Facius' achievements in Hesse became particularly noteworthy to Simolin while at the same time attracting the suspicions of the local magistrates.

In a letter to the government of Hesse-Darmstadt on February 7, 1766, the Councellor-President of Mainz, Friedrich Karl Joseph van Erthal, wrote:

> According to reliable reports, emmissaries...are busily recruiting many of our country's subjects to go to foreign colonies. They are successful by picturing untrue advantages, in gaining large crowds of colonists...who soon go to ruin...Since, however, the country is in danger because of this disadvantageous depopulation; we deem it necessary for the preservation of our country's welfare...that the harmful recruiters be prevented from carrying out their intentions as soon as possible.[32]

The Hessian government concurred in a letter of reply on February 24, 1766, adding that it would "instruct each and every official to meet this evil with great care and diligently further recruitment."[33] Accordingly, edicts forbidding emigration and threatening emigrants with the expropriation of the possessions were issued in Mainz on February 18, by the Prince of Nassau-Weilburg on April 12, and by the Mayor and Council of the Free City of Frankfurt a.M. on April 21. Concerted action was taken similarly by the princes of the Lower Rhine and in the province of the Palatinate and on April 28 by the Landgrave of Hesse.[34]

In such pronouncements the activities of the agents for settlement in Russia were variously labelled *das verderbliche Unheil* (the pernicious disaster), *einer Menschen Handel* (a slave trade), and a trade dealing with people *wie mit dem Viehe* (as though they were cattle.)[35] In some cases advocating the arrest and execution of the offenders, Simolin sought to arbitrate the matter through the proper diplomatic channels while suggesting to Facius in Frankfurt that he "quietly and well ahead of time" find a more secure place to reside in the area.[36]

Various court-appointed investigators made journeys throughout Hesse to ascertain the nature of the problem, finding much of the citizenry still resolved to emigrate due to the pressing economic situation; particularly distressing conditions prevailing from the Odenwald to Vogelsberg areas. Official recommendations to eliminate servile tributes, establish food repositories, and reduce interest rates on loans were destined by government officials who chose to advocate a less costly and inadequate solution of "honest work and diligence."[37]

After considerable effort following his expulsion from Frankfurt, Facius succeeded in relocating his operations to Büdingen, the capital of the small Duchy of Isenburg located northeast of Frankfurt a.M. near the hilly Vogelsberg area.[38] In this relatively isolated area Facius received an overwhelming response at a time when a Hamburg official of the Tutel-Kanzlei ordered him to "halt the sending of more colonists for the year entirely."[39] Simolin immediately filed a vehement objection to Catherine II herself upon learning of Facius' embarrassing position in Büdingen where scores of Germans were preparing to leave and were living in the city on crown subsidies.[40] The entire issue of curtailing the program at this point was contrary to Simolin's personal plans to establish a continuing ordered flow of European colonists to develop the Russian's vast agricultural and industrial potential. However, bureaucratic difficulties in the Tutel-Kanzlei with the settlement program for the vast empire were becoming increasingly apparent and heavy foreign diplomatic pressure was now being exerted in St. Petersburg.

Though Simolin's intervention allowed Facius to continue his operations in Isenburg throughout the summer of 1766,[41] the Russian government arranged for the publication of a decree in German newspapers in September, 1766, warning that "in the year following 1766, settlers would no longer be accepted" and they were exhorted not to be deceived into "making agreements with persons independently assembling settlers." A dispatch the previous June received by Simolin from the Russian vice-chancellor, Nikita Panin,[42] directed him to "limit himself to sending only the settlers who have

39

already been accepted and who cannot be decently discharged."[43] The significance of this action is evident in that most of the Volga German colonists in Russia that ultimately immigrated to America's Pacific Northwest descended from those recruited by Facius in Büdingen in the summer of 1766.

When promised a subsidy for the use of his capital as Facius' new *Sammelplatz* for organizing emigrant caravans, the Duke of Isenburg in Büdingen reciprocated by promising to "afford every assistance" to him.[44] A guarantee was secured against what often resulted in inflated prices under such conditions for food, provisions, wood, straw, and other supplies. Simolin was soon reporting that "Commissioner Facius, having now changed his place of residence from Frankfurt to Büdingen, cannot find words to adequately praise the goodwill and friendliness which the ruling family there has shown, both to him personally and in the matter of the settlers, on the recommendation of my letter." He further stated that in order to "accomodate the colonists, he was given the use of the local town-hall and another large public building, and if they found these too crowded, he was allowed to quarter the settlers in the house of any citizen. Bakers, butchers, and brewers were ordered to provide sufficient edible provisions and to sell these for a fair price." The general public was ordered not "to lend anything to a settler, and if he did, no complaints would be dealt with." According to Simolin, the "ruling Duke of Isenburg-Büdingen himself made it clear to the commissioner that if he experienced any difficulties, he was to apply directly to him."[45]

Facius sent the first group of settlers from Büdingen to Lübeck between February 25 and March 6, 1766. The Germans moved overland through Schlitz, Cassel, and Hildesheim to the port city of Lübeck, a journey involving approximately 500 people per trek.[46] As the party moved through these towns, it was not uncommon to attract the interest of others who joined the groups of immigrants bound for the Volga region. In Lübeck they boarded ships and began their long arduous journey to their new home in Russia. Once on Russian soil, the Germans acquired wagons which they loaded with their goods and their families. Thus, they began their movement through and lives in their adopted country of Russia. A typical column departing Büdingen in the summer of 1766 consisted of eighty families from some thirty-seven villages in Vogelsberg and neighboring areas who would ultimately found the Volga colony of Jagodnaja Poljana (Beerenfeld) the following year.[47]

These renewed activities elicited two divergent responses in the surrounding provinces where the emigration had been officially curtailed. Such appeals as the following addressed to the landgrave of Hesse-Darmstadt drew the sympathies of some and the condemnation of others.

> We the following people are as a whole all so reduced in circumstances that we for that reason are prepared to take a beggar's staff, because even our few possessions have debts and we cannot support ourselves. For that reason we have decided to travel to the Russian Empire with others. Most esteemed landgrave, most gracious prince and master, I Johann Hofmann, myself and family, Johannes Bechtold with wife and children have been arrested and put in a state of serfdom to you lordship and because of this and to be permitted to leave the country we need your gracious dispensation. We, therefore, ask your princely serene Highness that you graciously grant our most subservient, humble and prostrate request to leave your princely lands. We comfort ourselves with the thought of a most gracious favorable hearing, etc.
>
> Johann Hofmann with wife and 5 children
> Johannes Bechtold with wife and 3 children
> George Michel Müller with wife and 2 children
> Johann Tobias Lentz with wife and 4 children
> Johannes Alten, widower with 5 children
> Von Eckhardsborn
> District Lissberg Superior
> Baliwick Nidda[48]

Such pleas were not isolated and evoked the sympathies of many officials. On March 7, 1766 the Hessian government in Giessen advised the landgrave in a report that it would not be harmful to the state to allow emigration in such cases where debt and poverty were the motivating circumstances as their efforts to mitigate these situations had been admittedly fruitless.[49]

Coupled with additional recommendations by other magistrates, principally the Elector of Mainz who demanded a

41

strict enforcement of the earlier legislation forbidding emigration altogether, the Hessian government sought a compromise. It released to its courts a statement dated April 11, 1766 ordering that permission to emigrate could only be given to those "indolent" persons who had paid all outstanding taxes and fulfilled their civil obligations, realizing that they would not be extended acceptance in the future should they ever desire to return. Likewise, anyone immigrating without permission from the government to do so was in danger of having all of their property and any remuneration for previously sold personal items confiscated by the government. Furthermore, the borders would be carefully watched to prevent anyone from leaving without proper authority, and anyone who observed and reported a Russian agent operating in Hesse-Darmstadt would receive a reward of twelve florins.[50]

Inevitably authorities in areas neighboring Isenburg began calling upon the government at Büdingen to expell Facius since their decrees, by nature difficult to adequately enforce, had not resulted in stemming the steady flow of their subjects to refuge in Isenburg. Throngs of people converged on the town and made preparations to depart, with 375 marriages taking place in the small village between February 24 and July 8, 1766.[51] Particularly incensed were officials in Hanau and Mainz who learned that twenty-five and twenty-two citizens from their cities respectively, had been illegally accepted into one of Facius' transports. Simolin attempted to arbitrate the dispute by ordering these forty-seven persons be excluded from the group enroute to Lübeck while Facius promised to add a special Isenburg government official to his staff in order to check the backgrounds of prospective emigrants.[52]

Nevertheless, in accordance with the instructions from the Empress, Simolin ordered Facius to attenuate recruitment and by the close of 1766 operations throughout Germany had virtually ended. It was, however, the culmination of one of the most successful efforts ever in a programmed migration with approximately 27,000 people emigrating to Russia's Volga region alone between 1763 and 1766.[53] Three thousand families of "crown" settlers were largely recruited by Facius alone, the remainder under the authority of proprietors.[54]

Although Catherine's original manifestoes regarding colonization indicated settlers would "be assigned to their destination according to their wishes and desires," she modified this clause through the Ukase of March 19, 1764, in which she appropriated lands in the Saratov province for their occupation, extending between the Volga and Medveditza Rivers from Volsk to Tsaritsyn. Later in the year and in 1765 she arranged proprietory grants on the east side of the Volga in the province of Samara. It was to these regions that the majority of the German colonists were directed and by the end of 1767 they had founded 104 colonies,[55] forty-four on the western *Bergseite* and sixty on the eastern *Wiesenseite.*

In Germany final action was taken to curb emigration as German princes prevailed upon Emperor Joseph II to issue an edict on July 7, 1768 prohibiting all such foreign activity in the remaining free cities of the Empire that harbored agents.[56] As the Russian government had already begun curtailing transport subsidies, only 604 persons managed to emigrate between 1767 and 1773.[57] These did so voluntarily and some founded the Volga colony of Pobotschnoje in 1772 while others were settled in colonies previously established on the Volga.[58]

Map. 2

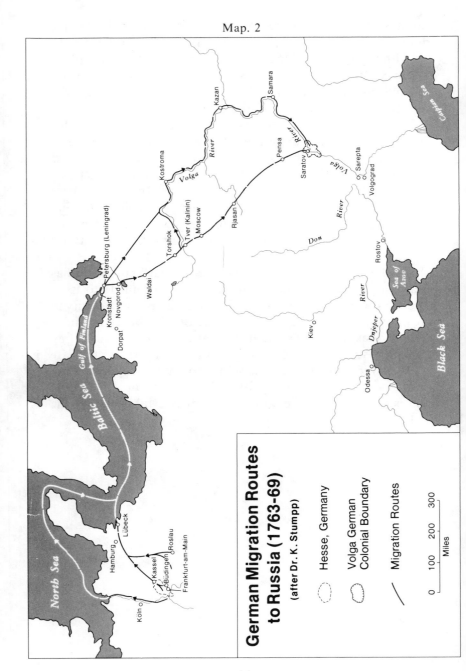

German Migration Routes to Russia (1763-69)

(after Dr. K. Stumpp)

◌ Hesse, Germany

○ Volga German Colonial Boundary

— Migration Routes

0   100   200   300
Miles

2

COLONIAL DEVELOPMENT
ON THE VOLGA

Wir verliessen unser
Vaterland,
Und zogen in das Russenland.
Die Russen war'n uns sehr
beneidt,
Und weil wir war'n so lan
befreit.

And so we left our fatherland,
To Russia then we moved, as
planned.
But jealous the Russians
turned out to be,
Because so long we had been
free.

—"Das Manifest," v. 2

The 900 mile voyage from Germany to Russia could normally be made in nine days although events often prolonged it to weeks and in one instance to nearly three months. For the most part the delays were unavoidable due to inclement weather or unfavorable winds, but often ship captains wanted to wait and sell their provisions at inflated prices as supplies diminished.[1] According to one German passenger,

The majority of us had never been upon a ship, it was hard for people to stand up because of the natural swaying of the boat. They tumbled against each other; fear and trembling mastered every mind; one cried, another swore, the majority prayed, yet in such a varied mixture that out of it all arose a strange and woeful cry.[2]

Reports on food and accomodations vary, some offering only praise for their treatment while others stated the only food available was salt, molded bread, and water.[3]

After arrival in Kronstadt, the Russian naval port on an island in the Gulf of Finland, the colonists were taken to the city of Oranienbaum (Lomonosov) on the mainland, the site of one of Catherine's royal residences. The German pastor of the Lutheran Church there would often lead them in the oath of allegiance to the Russian Crown. Catherine herself sometimes went there personally to welcome the colonists in their native tongue. Many of them had intended to pursue their trades near St. Petersburg but most were compelled by Guardianship Chancery officials to join the others in developing the agricultural districts on the lower Volga. The colonists often remained in Oranienbaum from two to six weeks while preparations were made for their trek to the Volga which could take place over various routes. Some crowded again into ships which took them up the Neva River past St. Petersburg to Schlüsselburg and down Lake Lagoda to Novgorod via the Volkov River. From there they traveled overland to Torshok on the Volga where ships transported them to Saratov from which the groups dispersed to the sites of proposed settlements.[4]

A second major route led entirely overland from Oranienbaum, the men on foot escorting wagons loaded with women. children, and provisions as they traveled southeast through Novgorod, Waldai, and Tver. At this point some traveled on barges down the Volga to Saratov while others continued overland through Moscow, Ryazan, Pensa, and Petrovsk to Saratov. Guided by Russian officers, the caravans traveled deep into the interior on the primitive roads that became nearly impassable in the fall and spring while the heavy Russian snows prevented travel by both river and land during the harsh winter months. While the advertisements had indicated such an excursion from St. Petersburg to Saratov could be accomplished in two to three weeks by land or from five to six weeks *zu Wasser auf dem Wolga,* in actuality it often took from nine to eighteen months for the settlers to complete the entire trip.[5]

During the coldest winter months the immigrants were quartered in the homes of Russian peasants in such villages as Torschok and Kostroma.[6] Under such circumstances it became necessary for them to adapt to the peasant diet consisting largely of cabbage soup, millet porridge, and kvas.[7]

46

Great distances remained to be covered after travel recommenced in the spring and many colonists finally reached their destinations on the Volga too late to plant their crops and many were compelled to eat the seed grain to avoid starvation.

The first contingent of German colonists arrived in the Volga settlement area to establish the village of Dobrinka, located near Kamyshin, on June 29, 1764. By the fall of the year additional expeditions founded Beideck, Shilling, Galka, and Anton. The steady stream of German settlers peaked in 1767 when sixty-eight colonies were founded including several that would contribute heavily to emigration from Russia to America's Pacific Northwest in the nineteenth century, most notably Kolb, Jagodnaja Poljana, Norka, Frank, Walter, Warenburg, and Hussenbach.[8] All were located on the *Bergseite,* two other villages there would also be involved in this later movement — Balzer, founded in 1765, and Messer (1766).

Since many had expected to find available materials and buildings constructed in anticipation of their arrival, the sudden termination of their journey on the broad unbroken steppe instilled in many a sense of utter abandonment. In the case of those who established Kratzke[9] in 1767, one of the colonists reported their response in the following words:

> Our guides call "Halt!" at which we were very much surprised because it was early to put up for the night; our surprise soon changed to astonishment and terror when they told us that we were at the end of our journey. We looked at each other, astonished to see ourselves here in a wilderness; as far as the eye could see, nothing was visible except a small bit of woods of grass, mostly withered and about three shoes high. Not one of us made a start to climb down from his horse or wagon, and when the first general dismay had been somewhat dissipated, you could read the desire in every face to turn back. This, however, was not possible. With a sigh, one after another climbed down, and the announcement by the lieutenant, given with a certain degree of importance, that everything we saw here was presented to us with the compliments of the Empress, did not produce in one of us the slightest pleasure. How could such a feeling have been possible, with a gift which was useless in its present condition and had not a particle of value; a gift that must first be created by us with great

47

toil and which gave no certain assurance that it would repay the labor and time spent upon it.

"This is truly the paradise which the Russian emissaries promised us in Lübeck," said one of my fellow sufferers with a sad face.

"It is the 'lost paradise,' good friend," I assured.[10]

The column of eighty families which had departed Büdingen in the summer of 1766 abruptly arrived at their destination forty miles northwest of Saratov on August 28, 1767.[11] Again the colonists were dumbfounded when they were commanded "Here you will stay!"[12] Without proper tools and implements it was impossible to cut lumber from the forest to the north or turn the virgin sod. Moreover, it was not believed that the spring there could support an entire colony.

So a few men took some arms and went north (about two miles)...and heard a strong roaring of water in a deep gorge, like a small waterfall. They worked their way through innumerable obstacles until they found it. Nobody had ever found this spring before them. Everybody agreed this was the place for their new colony...Jagodnaja Poljana (Berry Meadow).[13]

As with other initial groups immigrating to a new colony, the problem of shelter became acute in a land where early winters strike with great severity. The settlers learned from the native Russians how to construct *zemlyanki,* or earth houses, which consisted of excavated pits covered with a roof made with wagon planks, limbs, and twigs and covered with a mixture of dry grass and mud. Most dugouts, particularly those constructed in low-lying areas or on river banks were threatened later by heavy spring runoffs. Marauding packs of wolves were to be a constant threat to the livestock and winter trips across the glistening steppes in troikas were sometimes interrupted by the descending predators. For this reason an extra horse or colt was often tied to the sleigh and released if necessary to deter their attacks.[14] The difficult plight of the German settlers, suffering from constant dampness in their earthen homes, led to an alarming mortality rate, which was particularly high among the infants. One of the original colonists, Anton Schneider, described the conditions. He stated that "throughout the winter we lived

48

miserably and in greatest need. The dark winter days and the eternally long nights seemed to last forever. We were separate from all other human beings, and in many cases did not even have enough to eat."[15]

The number of German colonist families on the Volga decreased from 6,433 in 1769 to 4,858 in 1775 and stability was not established until 1785.[16] Russian German historians came to term the period between 1765 and 1775 "*Die Jahre der Not.*"[17] In many cases it took several years before the townsites could be platted and the blocks sectioned off into homesites. Some homes were built with bricks formed from loam mixed with straw and covered with pole framed, thatched roofs. Rectangular wood dwellings were later constructed parallel to the street as the building materials became available, typified by an enclosed central entryway opposite the street side leading into the summer kitchen. Two nearly identical rooms flanked the entryway which were the living quarters for the extended family. Furnished simply, each room usually held two or three beds, a table and benches for eating, and a wall cabinet holding the wooden spoons, bowls, Bible, and other necessary items. The farmyards were arranged six to a block, usually about 125 feet wide and nearly twice as long and were divided into front and rear portions (*Fehderhof* and *Hinnerhof*). The former was a fenced compound within which was the family home, barns, equipment sheds, root cellar, and fireproof hut to protect valuables. In the *Hinnerhof* the family maintained a large vegetable garden and several fruit trees. Wooden granaries were also often built there to escape damage in case of a house fire.[18]

Most Volga German villages had a single main street and several parallel and cross streets with the church and school at the center of the community. Certain streams, wells, stone quarries, sand pits, and hardpan deposits for whitewash were held for use by all residents of the colony. Woodlands were protected though certain areas were periodically opened for cutting. Apiaries were established in some colonies with the hives often formed out of hollowed tree trunks. Families farmed their eighty acre allotments in the outlying areas but rarely lived apart from the colony. In later years, it often became necessary for some to lease or extend operations to lands located on the periphery of the colony's domain. In such instances a *khutor*, or self-sustaining settlement, was established often composed of a dozen or more families.

In addition to the natural calamities associated with their early settlement, conflicts with the indigenous peoples of the Volga also stalled colonial development. Bands of escaped Russian serfs and fugitives stalked the region, attacking and robbing the German colonists. The nomadic Mongol tribes of Kirghiz and Buddhist Kalmyks looked with suspicion upon the encroaching settlers. As early as 1764, the German colonists were assailed by these marauders who sought money, provisions, livestock, and in some cases enslaved their captives. The Kirghiz became particularly adept at horse raiding and wreaked devastation on a wide scale on the *Wiesenseite* beginning in 1771, particularly in villages along the Great and Little Karaman Rivers. Such depredations continued for over a century and as late as 1882 nearly 10,000 horses were reported stolen during the previous eight-year period on the east side as well as innumerable cattle and sheep.[19]

Insight into the gradually improving conditions on the *Bergseite* is reflected in the following letter, few of which survive since the primitive postal services severly restricted communication with the German homeland. Written in January, 1774 by Johann Heinrich Kühn of Beideck, the letter was sent to his relatives in Hesse describing his journey and conditions of settlement. After praising God, "who has shown me and my loved ones so much grace," he thanked his "dear Saviour" who had "torn us out of earthly poverty and transformed us to a land and climate where we have nothing more to complain about than our physical needs." Kühn reported "that we have a climate suitable for growing and the soil is fertile. We can write this in truth — everything can be raised here, corn, wheat, barley, oats, peas, lentils, millet, potatoes, tobacco,...watermelons, melons and cherries." Not only was he encouraged by the possibilities of production, but he was likewise excited about the marketing possibilities of these and other crops, including hay, cabbage, cucumbers, and other

50

vegetables. Kühn was convinced that livestock thrived in the natural habitat along the Volga, and in particular he felt that hogs, horses, cows, oxen, chickens, and geese did well in the region. He believed that the Germans who had moved to Russia had made the correct decision, and he wrote exclaiming:

> When we, dear friends, think back to our fatherland, what a great change now has taken place in the meantime, how we were burdened down with work and ate our bread in tears but now have been set in material and mental security — for which I and my dear wife and children want to give thanks our whole life.
>
> Our great monarch cared for us at our arrival with a real mother's heart. Our great Empress as long as we can breathe, that our dear Savior will bless her to the thousandth generation and grant all inhabitants peace and tranquility.[20]

By the following summer, however, whatever tranquility existed in the Volga German colonies was shattered by one of the greatest peasant revolts in Russian history. Beginning in the autumn of 1773, the Don Cossack, Emelian Pugachev, led the insurrection, posing as the escaped and still reigning true Tsar of Russia, Peter III, who intended to punish his wife Catherine II. He promised freedom from serfdom and taxation and called for the extermination of civil officials and landlords. Within months the rebellion attracted thousands of serfs, factory workers and miners, Old Believers, Tatars, Bashkirs, and others who descended in a massive campaign southeast from Petrovsk toward Saratov in the first week of August, 1774. On August 5, Jagodnaja Poljana was attacked, three men were captured and later whipped to death.[21] The following day Saratov was taken and the rebels ransacked the city, opening prisons, government storehouses and executing captured aristocrats and officials whose bodies Pugachev ordered left unburied.[22] After three days he led his forces down along the west bank of the Volga through the German villages which he left ravaged and in ashes.

Many settlers fled to hide in the countryside, burying what few valuables they possessed while others remained in the villages. One such individual, Johann Wilhelm Stärkel, great-grandfather of Reverend Wilhelm Stärkel who was a leading figure in the later pietistic movement, was seized by

51

Pugachev's men when they entered the colony of Norka. Along with others he was forced to drive the rebels' stolen wagons to a point near Kamyschin and later miraculously escaped.[23] Continuing to sweep southward, the main force under Pugachev passed through Dönnhof and approached Kratzke where "cellars, and clay pits and even wells were filled with all kinds of property and strewn with earth. The cattle were driven into the forests and canyons or tied among the reeds and rushes of the river."[24]

A young man, hiding with others in the garret of the Kratzke schoolhouse, later related how Pugachev arrived in front of the school in a heavily escorted carriage and promptly had a gallows erected from two long poles and a crossbeam. Four bound prisoners on horseback were led in and beaten, then hung in pairs on two ropes thrown over the crossbeam.[25] The grim scene was repeated many times as surviving colonists recalled the times when at night the horizon was bright with the lurid flames of destruction in the villages. Pugachev was finally defeated by government forces south of Sarepta and was later captured following his betrayal by fellow rebels. He was taken to Moscow where after a trial, he was executed.

Such violent episodes were rare in the isolated Volga colonies and their location prevented any direct involvement in the European wars of the period. However, following the debacle of Napoleon's invasion of Russia in the Franco-Russian War of 1812, many German-speaking prisoners of war from Lorraine, Switzerland, Mainz, Brunswick, and other powers allied with Napoleon were sent to the Volga colonies for internment. Weary of the endless wars being waged on the continent, many chose to marry into local families and begin new lives among the secluded colonists.

Following the difficult period of adjustment and drought, economic prosperity steadily developed in the Volga colonies, especially in the realm of agricultural production. This was particularly evident on the *Bergseite* where the black chernozem soil was highly organic and often three to five feet deep. This region is among the most fertile in Europe although the soil becomes more chestnut-brown in color further south on both sides of the river, deteriorating into the semidesert conditions of the upper Caspian depression.[26]

Apart from the old center of trade and industry for the Volga colonies, Saratov, the village of Sarepta, founded on September 3, 1765 developed into an important industrial center. Settling over 150 miles below the original colonial enclave's southern boundary, Moravian Brethren in Sarepta introduced the manufacture of sarpinka, a choice cotton material, to the region.[27] The economic achievements of this industry gained the attention of the Guardianship Chancery, where the authorities were quick to point out their success to other Russian officials. The production of the cloth soon expanded to Norka, Messer, Balzer, Katharinenstadt, and elsewhere and was exported throughout the empire, Sarepta becoming a show-place for visiting government bureaucrats and delegations.

Virtually every German colony contructed a flour mill for local consumption, most on the western side initially powered by water from the abundant streams while settlers on the eastern plains side fashioned Dutch-type windmills. Technically owned by the colony, management of the mills was awarded on a bid basis with these funds used to operate the school system and other public services in the village. Oil mills were also widespread in the colonies as it was found that the tall sunflower stalks grew well in the area and the crushed seeds from the broad yellow heads yielded a high quality cooking oil while the refuse was fed to the livestock.[28] Tanning and tobacco industries also developed. The hilly prairies of the *Bergseite* were well-suited to cattle production while tobacco growing and pipe manufacturing were largely confined to the *Wiesenseite*.

Balzer became an important commercial center for the Volga colonies, its fabric dyeing establishments, founded in 1840, contributing to the prosperity of its textile mills.[29] At one point the city boasted of two oil mills, a foundry and machine factory, two clothing factories, seventy-two sarpinka factories with fourteen thousand looms, fifteen dyeing houses, seventeen tanneries, twelve pelt factories, twelve smitheries, and numerous other enterprises.[30]

53

The vast majority of colonists, as many as 97 per cent, remained farmers. The first decade of despairing crop yields ended in 1775 when the cycle of rainfall ended the period of drought and adequate rains fell throughout the region. In addition the virgin acreage could be brought under greater cultivation as colonial smiths replaced the crude Russian *sokhi* or iron-tipped wooden plows. The settlers introduced German moldboard plowshares which, when used singly or joined in pairs, could penetrate deeper and turn larger tracts of the heavy sod. Cultivation improved with iron harrow teeth and other implements and many colonists became adept at breeding quality draft horses to pull tillage equipment.

The colonies found it impractical to farm intensively since large areas were opened for them to cultivate. Commercial fertilizing techniques were unknown but they did practice three and four-year crop rotation. A typical field cycle might rotate from rye one year to sunflowers and potatoes the next. This land was summerfallowed during the third year until sown back to rye. Several vast fields were maintained surrounding each colony to insure that adequate supplies of each commodity would be produced annually.[31]

Farm work began every spring as the melting snows revealed a lush growth of winter rye covering at least one of the large colony fields. As the Volga Germans consumed rye flour heavily, it became the most important cereal grain raised in the colonies. It was generally planted in late August following summer rains while crops more susceptible to winter kill — sunflowers, spring grains, and potatoes — were planted in late March and April. Both soft and hard varieties of spring wheat were raised although hard wheat grew in demand, due to its high protein and gluten content, and was commonly raised as a cash export crop.[32] Millet, the third major grain raised in the colonies, was also sown in the spring and was used in making *Hirsche,* a coarse porridge. Oats and barley, both used chiefly as animal fodder, were also spring crops.[33]

Care was taken in the preparation of seed grain to insure that it was free of weed seed and uncracked. This was accomplished by running the bulk grain from the previous

54

harvest through both a fanning mill and a special sieve. The seedbed was often prepared by breaking the previously plowed ground with a crude triangular-shaped cultivator pulled by a team of horses. This was followed by pulling a ten to fifteen foot long roller which crushed the clods and packed the ground to conserve moisture.[34] Sowing was by hand broadcast which was sometimes followed by a light harrowing. Sunflowers were planted by hand in alternate furrows during spring plowing, the successive rounds with the single or double share plow covering the preceding planting. Potatoes were planted in the same manner. It was exhausting labor that demanded skillful handling of the draft horses and careful measuring of the distance between seeds by those planting throughout the long day. At the same time others planted the large communal melon and cabbage gardens while women planted their other vegetables in the *Hinnerhof.*[35]

In late spring the settlers turned their attention to the manufacture of *Mistholz* (manure wood), an economical fuel developed by the Volga Germans which prevented the destruction of their dwindling woodlands. Barnyards were usually cleaned weekly and the refuse deposited in one corner of the yard or, more commonly, at one of several places on the outskirts of the colony near a stream. Families gathered to prepare the *Mistholz* by adding water and straw to a layer of manure which was spread out over a hard flat surface. Horses were then led around several times to mix the mass. It was allowed to dry in the hot sun in large rectangular molds or cut into blocks with a spade and piled for use in winter as an odorless slow burning fuel.[36]

In May the colonists busied themselves by repairing their homes, mills, and farmyard buildings. Most houses received an annual coat of whitewash mixed from chalky soil near the village. This was also the time to cut the wild grasses which grew in the communal meadows in order to augment the winter hay supply. Following this it was necessary to hoe the vegetable crops in the fields and gardens while the livestock was turned out to graze on the volunteer grain growing in the

55

fallow fields. In June spring plowing commenced on lands that would remain idle until sown to rye.

It was not unusual for the colonists to find that their stores of rye were entirely depleted by early summer. It was often necessary, therefore, to cut a few bundles of rye ripening in the fields late in June or early in July. These bundles were allowed to dry for at least two weeks and then flailed to get several bushels of the grain. Rye was the first grain to mature and was usually ready for harvesting in mid-July. Prior to the introduction of mechanical binders early in the twentieth century, the rye was cut with sickles which the government had distributed in the colonies soon after their settlement. However, pioneer ingenuity led them to fashion larger sythes equipped with cradles in order to cut and windrow in one movement.

Great dexterity was demonstrated by the women who followed the men to gather the cuttings into bundles which were tied together with several lengths of skillfully twisted and knotted rye stalks. The bundles were then collected into shocks for aeration which were carefully arranged into long rows. A patter of thousands of shocks (Kopitzen) was soon visible on the hills dotting the landscape around the colony. At the same time the vast expanse of bright yellow sunflowers came into full bloom as they followed the sun's path during the warm daylight hours.[37]

The next stage of the harvesting process involved the preparation of a threshing floor (Den or Tenne). This was usually located near the outskirts of the town at a designated area where each family was given a small area to stack their bundles for threshing. A team of horses was led around an area about fifty feet in diameter to flatten the surface. The area was then watered down and sprinkled with straw to form a hard surface. After two to three weeks of drying, the bundles were hauled to the threshing site by wagon. Several bundles at a time were then arranged side by side in a short row where a group of four or six adults stood on both sides to flail them. In large scale operations, dozens of bundles were spread out in a circular pattern to be threshed in a manner similar to that done with wheat later in the summer.[38]

Rhythmic folk songs were often sung by the workers as they set a tempo for swinging the long wooden flails. A narrow leather strap bolted on the end of the flail handle connected to a cylindrical piece of wood about a foot long. The bundles were then turned over and struck several times again and then opened for a final beating. Others lifted the stalks with wooden forks and stacked them for horse and cattle fodder. Until the middle of the nineteenth century, the colonists had to clean the threshings by tossing them into a crosswind by hand or with special wooden scoops to separate the slender brown kernels from the chaff in the ancient manner.[39] This technique continued until about 1840 when fanning mills were introduced in the colonies. This made it more practical for the farmers to thresh the grain as it was needed, especially for those who did not have their own granaries. It was not uncommon to see families busy in winter flailing rye on a hard layer of ice in the *Fehderhof.* Families with granaries could store all their rye during the winter but, since these were built off the ground to prevent mice infestation and moisture damage, they also risked the loss of some grain by theft as holes could easily be drilled through the wooden flooring.

The first spring crops to mature, oats and barley, were usually harvested in late July. Both were cut and stacked in the barnyard for the animals. This was followed by the threshing of millet. The production of hemp and flax, gathered in late summer, had been introduced by the *Tutel-Kanzlei* to fill the domestic needs of the colonists. After the heads were cut and beaten into a silken mass, they could be spun on a wheel into large balls which provided the women with material to fashion clothes during the long winter months.

By August the wheat fields maintained by the colonists were sufficiently ripened under the hot sun of the Volga summer to begin their harvest. The grain had to be threshed as soon as possible to avoid hail or fire damage. The farmers also dreaded the withering effects of a *Höhenrauch,* a searing hot dry wind from the southeastern desert region which could drastically reduce yield by shriveling the kernels and parching the ground.[40]

All able-bodied members of the family took part in the harvest work which began as early as two o'clock in the morning with the move out to the fields in the countryside. Wheat was principally an export crop although some white flour was used in making delicious fruit pastries (kuchen) and other foods. Wheat was often raised on acreages distant from the village on lands rented from wealthy Russian landlords on a fifty percent commission basis. The family would sometimes remain *"in dem Khutor"* for the entire week, living in tents if houses were not built, and returning to the village only on Saturday evening to prepare for worship on Sunday when all but the most essential labor ceased.[41]

A circular threshing floor was again prepared, though as wide as 150 feet, at a central location on the family's property. Again the brittle stalks were cut and bundled, but then brought directly by wagons to the threshing site. As many as two hundred bundles were then arranged into a circle along the perimeter of the *Den* and opened. A team of horses was led over the grain to "ride it out" of the heads. As with rye, the stalks were turned several times with wooden forks then vigorously shaken, raked aside, and stacked. Meanwhile, others would scrape the golden particles and chaff into a pile in the center of the ring. By late afternoon as many as 300 bushels of wheat had accumulated which were then winnowed and sacked in a process that often lasted until ten o'clock at night. Adequate supplies of grain were stored for seeding purposes and domestic use, and an amount proportional to the size of the family was deposited in the local *Grossambar,* a communal grain reserve, for emergency use. For this reason the Volga Germans were able to avoid famine until the Soviet period despite periodic crop failure.[42]

About the same time that winnowing mills were introduced to the colonies (c. 1840), "threshing stones" also came into use which were much more efficient than merely leading horses through the pilings. The stones were long sandstone rollers with canted grooves which revolved in a wooden frame as they were pulled by a team of horses.

Mechanical reapers and binders were not introduced until late in the nineteenth century and the revolutionary steam-powered stationary threshing machines appeared about 1910.[43]

Harvesting operations in August were often interrupted by summer rains which enabled the farmers to plant their winter rye while the standing grain dried. Planting took place on lands that had been spring plowed. Broadcasting continued to be the principal method of seeding in the colonies until American-made mechanical drills were made available to them just before the First World War. The farmers also began to turn the stubble on the recently harvested rye fields since these would later rotate to support spring crops.

The sunflower harvest usually began in early September. The four-foot high stalks were cut two rows at a time before the plump seeds became too brittle and were arranged in long rows with all the heads lying in the same direction. They were allowed to dry for about two weeks, during which time fall plowing continued. The stalks were then carefully placed on both sides of a wagon drawn between the rows. For this work the farmers sought oddly shaped branches in the timber which could be fashioned into four-pronged wooden forks. These resembled pairs of open claws on the end so that the stalk piles could be speared and placed with the heads in the middle of the wagon.

The wagons were then taken to the prepared threshing floor and the loads dumped so that the heads remained in the middle of the pile. It was extended into a row about a foot high and the heads either flailed or pounded with a wooden paddle. The stalks were turned three or four times, shaken and then raked away on both sides into a large stack. This was then hauled home and used as a secondary fuel source and some were saved for extracting a type of baking soda. The seeds were run through a fanning mill and the chaff and leaves saved to feed the sheep.

Sunflower seed generally commanded a high price on the Volga since it yielded a high quality cooking oil that was processed in the *Oehlemüle* (oil mills) located throughout the region. Sold by weight, the farmer's crop could be docked if it

59

was too damp. Late harvesting sometimes resulted in a high moisture content so a drying process was devised in which hundreds of pounds of seeds were spread out on a large canvas. Old men and children would then walk barefoot through the mass to keep it stirred and aerated. A penalty could also be imposed at sale if the sample taken indicated that too much dirt had "accidently" been sacked with the seed during the threshing operation.[44]

Potatoes were the last major crop to be taken in and these formed a major part of the Volga Germans' diet. They were dug with steel-tined forks and tossed into wagons in an arduous operation that continued for days. The potatoes were then dumped in small piles behind the houses to dry and put in a root cellar where they would be stored through the winter. Irregular blocks of ice insulated with straw and chaff usually lined portions of the large cellars so that dairy products and fresh meat could be stored there during the hot summer months. These chunks were collected early in the year along the banks of rivers and mill ponds after the spring thaw.

After the potatoes were dug, the families began gathering the cabbages, melons, and pumpkins which grew in the large communal gardens located on choice lands adjacent to the village. Sauerkraut was another staple food for the Volga Germans and was prepared immediately after the fall cabbage harvest. Melons were often packed in grain bins for storage. A delicious syrup was made by the women from ripe watermelons, though some were picked while small to be pickled in brine. Pumpkins provided a minor food source and the large seeds were often roasted to create a nut-like treat while the discarded shells were fed to the hogs. Garden vegetables commonly grown in the *Hinnerhof* included carrots, onions, and sugar beets which could be buried in a sanded corner of the root cellar for winter use. Tomatoes clinging to pulled vines often lasted through fall when hung in the cellars while cucumbers were crocked with dill or sweetened.

Apple, pear, and cherry trees were planted in both family gardens and in large communal orchards. Most fruits were

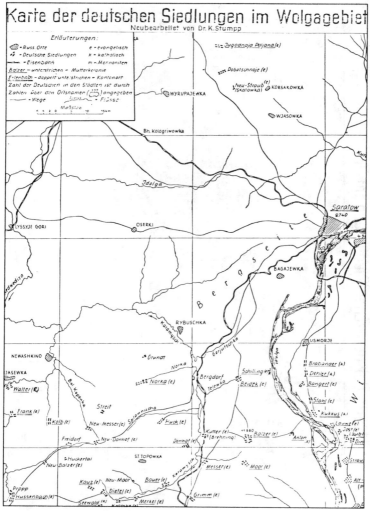

Map 3. The German settlements on the Volga (Bergseite).

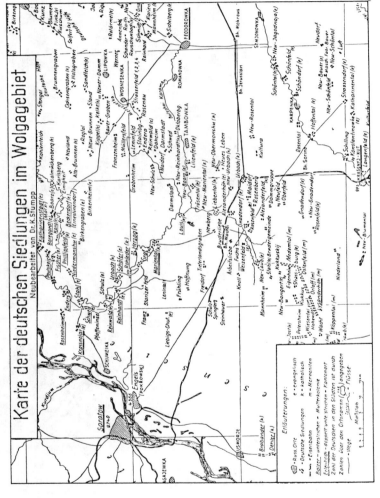

Map 4. The German settlements on the Volga (Wiesenseite).

Street

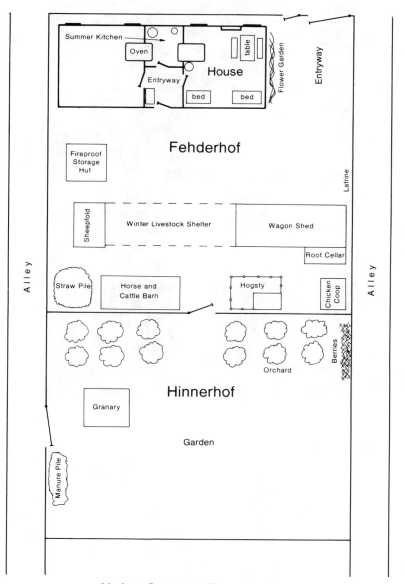

Volga German Farmyard

Map 5. Volga German farmstead.

Fig. 8. Emelian Pugachev, Cossack rebel leader.

Fig. 9. Vessels arriving at St. Petersburg.

Fig. 10. Russian village on the road between Novgorod and Tver.

65

Fig. 11. Volga River near Saratov. (Dr. Karl Stumpp)

Fig. 12. Plowing with the traditional Russian *sokha*.

Fig. 13. Balzer farmyard and panorama. (Dr. Karl Stumpp)

Fig. 14. Jagodnaja Poljana, Russia. (Mrs. John Bafus)

Fig. 15. Street scene in Messer, Russia. (Dr. Karl Stumpp)

Fig. 16. Russian German women flailing hemp (AHSGR)

69

Fig. 17. Shocks of grain or *Kopitzen*. (Dr. Karl Stumpp)

Fig. 18. Threshing with stone rollers.

Fig. 19. A winnowing mill. (Dr. Karl Stumpp)

Sammlung

Christlicher

Lieder

für die

öffentliche und häusliche Andacht,

zum Gebrauch

der deutschen evangelischen Kolonien an der Wolga.

Sechzehnte verbesserte Auflage.

———◦⋄◦———

Moskau.

Buchdruckerei von C. Liessner & J. Roman, Arbat, Haus Platonow.

Fig. 20. *Christlicher Lieder* songbook.

Fig. 21. Church and school in Frank, Russia.

Fig. 22. Interior view of the church in Balzer, Russia
decorated for Pentecost.

73

Fig. 23. Church in Norka.

Fig. 24. Tsar Alexander II, 1818-1881.

Fig. 25. Tsar Nicholas II, 1868-1918.

preserved simply by sun-drying although apples were sometimes pickled for consumption later in the year. Wild pear trees were common and wild strawberries and other berry varieties ripened as early as June while August showers sprouted succulent mushrooms.[45] Licorice root was gathered in the fall to be used in making the preferred Volga German drink — hot *Steppetee.* Volga German dinners typically consisted of nutritious combinations such as *Schnitzel Suppe und Kartoffel Wurst* (fruit soup and potato sausage), *Kraut und Brei* (sauerkraut and pork ribs) or *Klees und Arbuza* (fried eggs and dough with watermelon).[46]

The large numbers of animals maintained by the colonists provided an adequate supply of fresh meat, milk products, and eggs. Grazing areas were set aside in close proximity to the village but wolves were a constant threat to the livestock. Separate herders *(Hirten)* were often appointed to safeguard the villagers' cattle, sheep, and swine which fed on nearby fallow land in the spring. Milk cows were returned every evening to the edge of town by the herders where they were then taken home by their owners.[47] When the fallow land was planted, the animals were moved to the forest where they foraged through the summer until fall when they were turned out to the recently harvested fields. The livestock wintered in the protected confines of the *Fehderhof* where large temporary shelters were often built for the cattle and horses. Grain straw and hay for winter feed was stored in the spacious lofts of these structures.[48]

Several families often joined together for the annual butchering bee which took place in November or early December. Fruit tree cuttings were slowly burned to smoke sausage and other meat products made by the colonists. These were hung on racks placed in the summer kitchen chimney for smoking and then stored in the granary or other dry place. One of the last tasks undertaken by the farmers before the heavy snows curtailed outside activity was the gathering of old timber in the forests to supplement the winter fuel supply.[49]

With the long harvest season over, fall plantings completed, and produce sold or stored, the villagers gathered to celebrate their bounty in an exuberant festival, the *Kerb*.[50] This event signaled an end to the field season as the people prepared for the long Russian winter. Isolated on the steppe, the Volga German villages quieted to self-sufficient passivity. Courtship began among young couples considering matrimony and this custom often culminated in a mass marriage ceremony conducted in the gaily decorated church at Christmastime.

Following the period of sharp population decline between 1765 and 1775, when the number of families decreased from an estimated 8,000 to 5,502, the population began to steadily increase, reaching 31,000 by 1788 and 39,193 in 1798.[51] The crown's plan of family allotments became increasingly complicated with each new generation. This required reapportionment within the limits of the colony's boundaries and in 1797 a new government survey was mandated which yielded a reduced allocation the following year of about forty-two acres (15.5 dessiantines) per male. Colonist grievances evoked a promise from the government to increase the total to twenty dessiantines, as had been the case after the 1788 revision. This was not fully accomplished, however, until 1835 when any benefits were virtually cancelled, since by then the prolific Germans' shares averaged only about fifteen acres (5.6 dessiantines). This diminished even further to a scant 10.3 acres (3.8 dessiantines) in 1850[52] and the population was still increasing, reaching 238,000 in 1865,[53] a growth ten fold larger than the number that settled on the Volga a century earlier.

Problems arising from land tenure plagued colonial administration and because the 1763 Manifesto's tax exemption period had expired, the colonists gradually adopted the native Russian institution of the *mir*[54] as a means of equitably resolving these matters and for orderly self-government. On March 12, 1812 they were officially given identical tax status as landed Russian peasants which required a tax levied equally on all the male "souls" *(dushi)* but remitted collectively from the village *mir*. It became convenient, therefore, to adapt land distribution in accordance with the *mir* system of repartional tenure *(obshchinnoe pol'zovanie)* in which the land was divided among the male

77

population in regular revisions and could not be sold or mortgaged. By 1816 the system was in general use throughout the colonies and usually incorporated into the administration of the daughter colonies.[55] Great care was taken during the periodic revisions to insure an equitable distribution of land. At these times a specified number of males, usually about twenty and invariably related to one another, joined together to form an economic unit. Each of the main colony fields was surveyed, divided, and marked into lots that were to be farmed by the groups. The size of the lots was sometimes proportional to the fertility of the soil which was usually divided into three classifications: good (fertile lowlands), medial (or steep), and poor (sandy or rocky areas). This guaranteed that each family would be provided with the spring crops and rye on variable soils and would have to maintain some summerfallow.[56]

A public lottery, attended by at least one representative from every unit, was then held to determine who would receive which land parcels. Each male within a unit was then delegated a specific number of shares in their lands. The procedure was as complicated as it was judicious since each individual held title to as many as sixteen or more small plots. In addition, the communal garden properties were similarly apportioned. The basic problem of inadequate land supply, however, was not alleviated and new difficulties involving changing lines of demarcation, family size, and composition and varying soil quality compounded matters for the growing Volga German populace.

The government's solution to the dilemma of a regressive land supply was simply to expand Volga German settlement to other crown domains and between 1848 and 1863, the colonists founded sixty-eight daughter colonies *(Tochter Kolonien)*. Most were located on the *Wiesenseite* where approximately 675,000 acres were appropriated in the Novousensk district in 1840. Of these colonies, over one-third were located along the Jeruslan River where residents of Jagodnaja Poljana founded Neu Jagodnaja (1855) and Schöntal (1857) while others from Pobotschnoje established Schöndorf (1855) and Schönfeld (1858). Rosenfeld, a daughter colony of

78

Norka, was established in this area in 1859 while others there included Neu Beideck (1858) and Neu Bauer (1859). Neu Balzer, Neu Messer, and New Dönnhof were founded in 1863 in an area between the Medveditza and Karamysh Rivers on the *Bergseite* close to their mother colonies. Neu Frank and Neu Walter were built on land grants near the Schtschlkan River on the *Bergseite,* and Neu Norka was founded further south near Kamyschin in 1855.[57]

It is significant that at least two Volga Germans chose to immigrate to the United States while others were moving to the daughter colonies on the *Wiesenseite.* Possibly the first two Volga Germans to live in America, Johann Adam and Matthias Repp, brothers from their native Jagodnaja Poljana, journeyed to America about 1855 and homesteaded southeast of Humboldt, Kansas. Soon after the outbreak of the Civil War, however, they decided to escape the panic and return to Russia to join their families who had since relocated to Neu Jagodnaja. In 1876, Johann Adam Repp returned to Kansas with his family, other relatives and over two hundred others aboard the *S.S. Mosel,* most from Neu Jagodnaja and Schöntal.[58]

Life in the daughter colonies strewn along the upper Jeruslan River was difficult for the early settlers. They traveled to the distant lands in large caravans of livestock and wagons laden with seed grains, farm tools, and domestic items. Crossing the broad Volga River was hazardous on primitive wooden ferries. The families had been compensated for the loss of their property rights in the mother colonies and had volunteered to colonize the newly opened areas. However, they found the soil on the eastern rim of the *Wiesenseite* to be less fertile and the climate more arid. Many feared the nomadic Kirghiz horsemen who frequented the treeless plain and the distance from the mother colonies and major Russian trade centers effectively isolated them.

Like their ancestors who had come from Germany several generations earlier, they first lived in dugouts or tents until permanent homes could be constructed. The basic building material in this area was adobe brick. To prepare these, a wide pit was dug to a depth of about three feet where a dense layer of clay was encountered. Water was poured into the pit and a horse was led around to create a thickened consistency. Straw was then mixed with the mass for resilency and it was poured into wooden forms approximately sixteen inches square and eight inches high. Both houses and barns were built out of this brick and were covered with a pole frame roof which was thatched with reeds. The interior remained remarkably warm in the winter and cool in the summer. A massive adobe oven was built near the center of the house which protruded from a separate fuel storage room where it was fired with *Mistholz.*[59] Lands surrounding these daughter colonies were divided according to the *mir* system and the communities were governed in the same manner as the mother colonies.

As noted previously, civil authority in the colonies had been defined by the decree of April 28, 1776 which established the Saratov Office of the Guardianship Chancery *(Vormundschafts Kontor).* The Kontor consisted of a "chief judge" *(Oberrichter),* two assistants, a secretary, translator, bookkeeper, and later, various other bureaucrats. Beseiged by the initial problems of settlement and drought relief, its first chief executive, General I.G. Rezanov, staffed the office largely with Baltic Germans who looked upon the Low German colonists with some condescension. In 1769 the Guardianship Chancery introduced a detailed directive, "The Instruction," which defined the role of the Kontor as arbitrator in criminal and civil disputes, regulator of the agriculture economy, and responsible for the collection of crown taxes — a provision that led to widespread graft among the bureaucrats. In addition, six district commissars were appointed to supervise the transition of the colonists to Russian society, increased in 1775 to thirteen to provide one for each colonial district.[60] Government on the local level was to be administered by an elected major *(Vorsteher* or *Schulze)* and two assistants *(Beisitzer)* who oversaw public propriety and enforced legislation.

Intended to be only temporary institutions, the Guardianship Chancery in St. Petersburg and Saratov Kontor closed in April, 1782 with colonist affairs being transferred to

80

the regional bureau of the State Economic Directorate in Saratov. The move proved to be premature. While the German colonists had become an integral part of Catherine's plan for exploiting and securing that region of the Empire, language difficulties and jurisdictional problems associated with the change exacerbated tensions between the Germans and the aloof officials in the directorate. The tsarina personally intervened again by appointing Privy Councillor K. I. Hablitz to investigate the situation. Not only had she already extended the ten-year moratorium on the repayment of government loans specified in the Manifesto by an additional decade but in 1782 Catherine reduced their total liability of over 5,000,000 rubles by nearly 46%.[61] However, the ambitious monarch suffered a stroke and died on November 17, 1796 without having time to act on Hablitz's recommendations for reform.

Paul I, Catherine's son and successor to the Romanov throne, followed tradition by marrying a German princess, and throughout his short reign (1796-1801) maintained great admiration for the colonists' character and ability, often to the chagrin of the Russian bureaucrats and intelligentsia. Following Hablitz's advice, the tsar reopened the Saratov Kontor on July 31, 1797 under the Jurisdiction of the Department of National Economy, Guardianship for Foreigners and Rural Husbandry, a ponderous organization evolving in 1802 into the Ministry of the Interior which became in 1866 the Ministry of Royal Domains. The subsequent reigns of Alexander I (1801-25) and Nicholas I (1825-55) were both characterized by continued benevolence toward the German *kolonisty,* a term denoting their distinct legal status as landed state peasants which continued on officially until the Ukase of 1871 which abolished the privileges granted through Catherine's Manifesto although its usage prevailed in general use until the Communist Revolution.

A series of directives known as the "Uniform Instructions for the Internal Organization and Administration" of the colonies was promulgated between 1801 and 1803 in an attempt to allow more effective self-government in the colonies and restore confidence to the newly reinstituted *Kontor* at the

81

community, district, and provincial levels. Locally, a village assembly *(Gemeinde/mirskoi skhod)* was formed, composed of one adult male representative from each household.[62] Additional provisions were made for an executive committee *(Kleingemeinde)* consisting of the Schulz and two assistants, elected by majority vote for two year terms, and a clerk *(Schreiber)*, a qualified hired official who maintained communication with officials in the next administrative level, the district *(Kreis)* which functioned as the intermediary between the Kontor in Saratov and the local *Gemeinden.*

Under the terms of the new legislation, however, the offices of appointed district commissars were abolished and substituted by an elected *Oberschulz (okruzhnoi golova)*, one for each of the ten newly-created Volga colony districts. Two or more elected assistants and an appointed district secretary *(Kreis Schreiber)* also served at this level, the chairman holding a three-year term and the assistants for two years. The district office was charged with the supervision of colonial farm management, it collected taxes and crown loan repayments and also served as a higher court for colonist litigation not resolved by the *Kleingemeide.*[63]

It was on the village level that civil responsibility and authority were particularly broadened as the functions of the *Gemeide* were enlarged and constables *(desiatski* or *sotniki)* were also elected to enforce the laws. At the village assembly, voting was done *viva voce* on such issues as the election of public officials, financial disbursements and local tax levies, distribution of surplus land and individual farmer assignments, crop rotation plans, the expulsion of citizens for immoral conduct, and confirmed the selection of teachers, pastors, fire inspectors, and village livestock herders.[64]

The pivotal figure in the adminstrative network was the mayor, a position that combined both civil and religious functions. His presence was required at the district meetings and he was responsible for seeing to it that taxes were paid promptly, buildings and homes were inspected to insure cleanliness and safety, everyone was diligent in church attendance, public morality was maintained by forbidding the sale of liquor to those "addicted to drunkedness, laziness and dissipation...(and that) every farmer began the day's work at sunrise."[65] Such indications of German industriousness and thrift coupled with the growing markets for grain in the mid-nineteenth century led to growing prosperity in the colonies. At that time, several western European nations, notably England, Belgium, and Holland, lowered and in some cases abolished tariffs on grain imports. Due to subsequent revisions in internal excise regulations, Russian markets substantially increased after 1860 commensurate with expansion in world demand.[66] During this same period, the activities of the *Kontor* at Saratov were gradually restricted and transferred to other provincial departments; by 1866 its functions were limited primarily to supervising the churches and schools in the colonies,[67] both of which faced serious difficulties.

Organizational problems had long been associated with the Lutheran Church in Russia, the inception of which can be traced back to the construction of a Lutheran Church in the German suburb of Moscow under the reign of Ivan the Terrible in 1576. The early expansion of the church was largely confined to urban areas in Russia where German artisans and technocrats were brought in by the tsars in efforts toward modernization. It was not until 1711 that Peter the Great appointed the first Superintendent of the Lutheran Church in Russia, Reverend Berthold Vagetius of Moscow, to preside over the activities of the ten parishes in Russia. The office was discontinued, however, following his retirement in 1718.[68]

New impetus was given to Protestantism in the predominantly Orthodox empire after 1763 when German Lutherans. Reformed and pietistic Moravian Brethren colonized the Volga region. Under the terms of the manifesto the colonists were allowed freedom of religion and were settled in villages according to their denomination. A principal reason for establishing the Moravian outpost at Sarepta was to proselyte among the Mongol tribes inhabiting that region and the Astrakhan steppe. Of the other Volga colonies, thirty-two were Catholic and seventy-two were Protestant with the majority (80%) being Lutheran; only seven Reformed villages were founded on the *Bergseite* where their two parish centers were at Norka and Messer while a number of Reformed villages were located on the *Wiesenseite* where a

83

minister was placed in Katharinenstadt, ministering at twenty-two locations!

Despite the great preponderance of Protestants, few pastors came or stayed with the colonists and due to the meager salaries of the clergy who were faced with ministering to scattered parishes often numbering over 2,000 souls, the lack of pastors became an acute problem. By 1805 there were only fifteen Protestant pastors in the entire colonial enclave, these living in Messer, Grimm, Beideck, Galka, Dietel, Frank, Norka, Stephan, Jagodnaja Poljana, Saratov, Rosenheim, Warenburg, Bettinger and two in Katharinenstadt.[69] The University of Dorpat (Tartu) in Estonia was the nearest theological school but the great distance and expense virtually prevented enrollment by eligible Volga German men.[70]

The shortage of clergy led to two significant developments in colonial Protestantism. Laymen of the congregations were increasingly compelled to handle spiritual matters themselves while between 1764 and 1825 the colonies witnessed an influx of Moravian Brethren missionaries from Sarepta.[71] Language problems and other difficulties with the Moravian missions to the Buddhist Kalmyks diverted their zeal to the Volga colonists in an attempt to justify the existence of their *Brüdergemeinde.* The Swiss Pietist Johann Janet began the work following a visit to Sarepta in 1766 when he enlisted the support of Johann H. Langerfeld for his church in Anton. Janet had been installed in the Reformed Church in Anton in 1765 after responding in Germany to their appeal sent the previous year soon after the colony was founded, many settlers having been acquainted with the work of the Brethren in Isenburg and other areas of Hesse and the Palatinate.[72]

Additional problems ensued as disputes arose between the growing pietistic Reformed elements and the rationalistic Lutheran leadership that rejected certain tenets of Calvinistic theology. They also differed in methods of distributing the elements at communion services and some Lutherans looked with suspicion upon local revivals, lay prayer meetings, and the personal lifestyle of piety. Nevertheless, the efforts of the Moravian missionaries met with a great response in many areas, particularly in Anton, Dietel, Balzer, and Dönhoff.[73]

Antagonisms between the two groups reached such proportions between 1818 and 1819 that government authorities in St. Petersburg decided to intervene. A decree was issued on October 25, 1819 establishing the Protestant Consistory for Inner Russia with headquarters to be in Saratov, from where a superintendent and staff would handle matters in all Protestant parishes throughout the entire empire.[74] The tsar appointed Dr. Ignatius Fessler head of the new Consistory. Fessler, formerly a Capuchin priest and oriental language professor, proved to be an effective organizer and sought to reconcile differences in Protestant Volga German clergy.

Fessler began by subdividing several parishes and personally recruiting new pastors from Germany — six in 1820 alone. At the same time he forbade missionary activity by the Moravians who withdrew their last evangelist, C. F. Lessing, in 1821.[75] He also fought tirelessly to obtain needed salary increases for the clergy and organized synod meetings for each side of the Volga and convened an annual general synod conference to discuss any problems confronting the churches. Further accomodation was reached through the publication of a common hymnal, the *Wolga Gesangbuch*,[76] and liturgical manuals acceptable to both Reformed and Lutherans, while preserving certain confessional variations. With the assimilation of the *Wiesenseite* Reformed parish into the larger Lutheran body in 1832 and the administrative union of the Norka and Messer Reformed parishes on the *Bergseite,* the title of the Protestant Consistory was altered to "Lutheran."

Among Fessler's most important contributions was organizing the struggling parochial school system of the colonies. Educational standards had severely declined due to financial problems and following the deaths of the original immigrant teachers as the colonies lacked teacher training institutes to prepare qualified educators despite numerous pleas by the colonists to the government. The situation in Norka was indicative of the eventual crises since at one time a single teacher supervised 1,100 pupils and was able to use only one large school room.[77]

Fessler responded by raising the issue of school reform at the meeting of the first general synod in January, 1822. Proposals were later enacted systematizing curriculums to include regular instruction in Bible history, Catechism, reading, writing, arithmetic, and music,[78] classtime usually amounting to three hours six days a week. Shifting frequently occurred in the morning and afternoon to accommodate a larger number of students. Maintaining the strict discipline characteristic of the system under the difficult circumstances required the services of an often stern and usually highly respected individual, the village *Schulmeister*. One of the few well educated members of the colony, he functioned as had been the case in Germany also, as church sextant *(Küster)* and registrar, all of these responsibilities being considered a single position. As the colony's pastor frequently ministered to other churches in the parish, he performed the necessary ecclesiastical duties and liturgical readings although only ordained men could preach from the pulpit.

In the congregation each woman, her head reverently covered with a beautifully embroidered or lace shawl *(Halstuck)*, sat with the smallest children on the left side of the church while the men and older boys sat on the right. The *Küster* also could not administer the Sacraments or baptize infants, unless in case of emergency.[79] He was authorized to conduct funeral services, usually held in the courtyard of the deceased following a two or three day wake *(Totewacht)* held in the home by the family. He also officiated at the internment rites which always concluded with the singing of *"Wo findet die Seele die Heimat der Ruh."*[80]

Fessler succeeded in convincing the government that it should permit the selection of schoolmasters by the parish pastor instead of the village assembly. This brought some ire from the colonists as did his attempts to obtain additional tax monies to remedy the deficiency in instructional materials, the number of teachers and their salaries, but these efforts were largely fruitless. Additional administrative reform coordinated terms of instruction in the Volga German *Volksschule* which had been largely confined to the winter months. School commenced in October and was extended usually until about

Easter when all laborers were needed at home and in the fields. Instruction generally began at age seven and continued eight years until at fifteen, following a detailed examination, the students were confirmed into full church membership in a grand and inspiring service held either on Palm Sunday *(Palmsonntag)* with communion on Good Friday *(Karfreitag)*, or at Pentecost *(Pfingsten)*.[81] Other festivals were celebrated in accordance with the liturgical church calendar including Easter *(Ostern)*, Ascension Sunday *(Himmelfahrt)*, Memorial Day *(Totenfest)*, Thanksgiving *(Danksagenfest)*, and Christmas *(Weinachten)*. In some colonies their original founders were honored in an annual *Herkommenstag*.

In 1832 the Lutheran Consistory was reorganized throughout the empire resulting in the interruption of Fessler's ambitious reforms. The main office in Saratov was suddenly shifted to Moscow which now became headquarters for the huge Moscow Consistory, one of eight major consistorial districts established by Nicholas I. These were all under the direction of a lay president of the General Consistory of the Lutheran Church in Russia, based in St. Petersburg. Each district was to have its own general superintendent and staff. The largest of the eight was the Moscow Consistory, serving scattered congregations stretching from Eastern Europe to Asiatic Russia, and it became necessary for effective organization to establish two sub-districts *(Propsteien)* for the Germans on the *Bergseite* and *Wiesenseite* of the Volga, each headed by a chief pastor *(Pröpste)*. With minor alterations this structure remained intact throughout the Tsarist period. However, the authority in religious matters had now been transferred to distant Moscow and the division of the colonies into separate entities further complicated efforts to solve mutual problems. Attempts to establish normal schools that could lead to adequate staffing in the parochial system failed and the lack of manpower continued to plague the clergy with pastors serving parishes averaging 6,592 people in 1861, swelling to nearly 13,000 in 1905.[82]

The appearance of two Moravian Brethren evangelists from Germany in 1868 in the Volga colonies marked the reemergence of pietistic fervor. Actually the activities of those influenced earlier by the missionaries from Sarepta had not been suspended despite Fessler's official termination of their efforts in 1820. On the contrary, a movement of the Brotherhood *(Brüderschaft)*, largely confined to the laity, continued to persist in the form of regular prayer meetings *(Versammlungen)* attended by many who objected to the liturgical formalism of the Lutheran Church. These sessions were often held secretly as they violated the Church Law of 1857 which decreed "that religious meetings which exceed the bounds of family devotions may hereafter not be conducted by laymen without previously notifying the civil authorities and obtaining permission from the Consistory."[83] The activities of the missionaries in 1868 were centered in the Reformed districts of Balzer and Messer where they gave new impetus to the movement, traveling widely in their trade as cobblers at the risk of public corporal punishment. Interest was kindled again in neighboring villages on both sides of the Volga and as far south as Dönhoff.[84] Expansion northward reached Pobotschnoje, Jagodnaja Poljana, and Katharinenstadt so that by 1872 the entire region was engulfed in a great revival that continued until the early 1890s.

It has been suggested that the official demurral expressed by the church against the pietists was due to its fear of the sectarianism that was being propagated by various cults on the Volga.[85] In order to disassociate themselves from such groups, the organization in 1871 of a non-sectarian Brotherhood Conference was effected in the village of Brunnental by the leaders of the movement. This was done in order to "consolidate the strength of the Brethren, to give them official recognition, to protect them against persecution, to provide a bulwark against Separatism and other sects, to clarify the doctrinal position of the converts, to set up rules for the individual prayer meetings, and to provide opportunity for mutual counsel and fellowship."[86]

The motivation force behind the Brotherhood's organization was the Reformed pastor from Norka, Wilhelm Stärkel, who had himself been converted in a revival meeting on the Volga. A brilliant organizer and inspiring preacher, he had traveled to Missouri and Kansas in the 1860s on a missionary journey. He returned in 1860 to serve a number of daughter colonies on the *Wiesenseite* until 1876 when he accepted a call to Norka.[87]

Religion played an extremely significant role in the lives of the Volga Germans, and religion would remain a central component of their social and cultural makeup throughout their history both in the Old and New Worlds. The roots of a separate denominational movement which characterized the lives of the Volga Germans in the Pacific Northwest emerged in Russia. Members of the Brotherhood expressed their theology in terms of a living dynamic expression of faith. While embracing traditional evangelical doctrines of the Trinity, universal priesthood of all believers, Biblical infallibility, and the Sacraments, they emphasized salvation by grace through the regenerative new birth experience. They taught that the Holy Spirit would then manifest itself in the believer's life through nonconformity to the world, involving a personal lifestyle of piety, prayers, study, and devotion to God. In addition, the Brethren were predominantly pre-Millennial, believing in the possibility of Christ's immediate bodily return to earth when he would gather His church to Himself. Their resolve to maintain church membership was equally evident. It was expressed on numerous occasions by one of their leading spokesmen, H.P. Ehlers, with the words *"Brüder, bleibt bei der Kirche."*[88] Ehlers and Johannes Koch were elected evangelists for the organization at the 1871 Conference.

Koch would later be instrumental in transplanting the movement to America's Pacific Northwest where the separate denominational movement arose — German Congregationalism. It has been suggested that one of the principal reasons for the burgeoning emigration of Volga Germans from Russia in the mid 1870s was the intolerant attitude of many toward the brethren.[89] One of the first Volga Germans to settle in the Pacific Northwest, George H. Green, was once flogged for protesting the punishment of a *Bruder* while others sympathetic to the movement were often made objects of ridicule and persecution.[90] It is significant that the first two groups of Volga Germans to the Pacific Northwest left Russia during this period and founded the first German Congregational Churches in the American West.

89

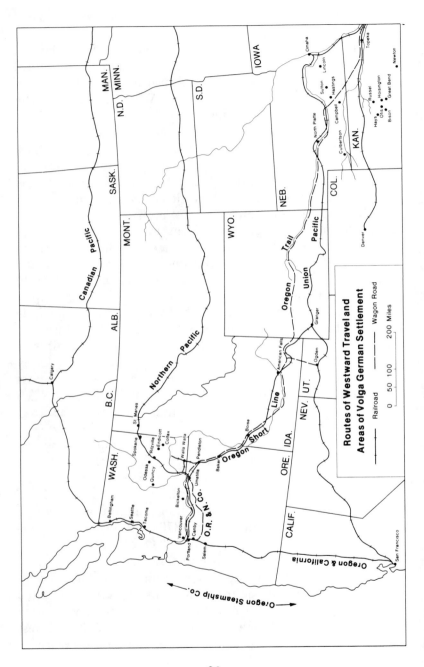

Routes of Westward Travel and Areas of Volga German Settlement

Railroad   Wagon Road

0 50 100   200 Miles

3

IMMIGRATION TO THE UNITED STATES

Hier in Russland ist nicht zu
leben,
Weil wir müssen Soldaten
geben,
Und als Ratnik müssen wir
stehen—
Drum wollen wir aus Russland
gehn.

Here in Russia it's no good
to live,
We must our men as soldiers
give.
And now as soldiers we must
stand,
That's why we leave the
Russian land.

— "Auswandererlied," v. 1

Ethnic German identity in the Volga colonies was increasingly threatened with the rise of the Slavophile movement in the 1840s and Pan-Slavism after 1870. Conceived among a group of romantic intellectuals during the reign of Nicholas I (1825-55), Slavophilism came to embrace a vision of the superior nature of the Orthodox Church and Slavic people. It held that they were on a supreme historical mission which would lead to peace and fraternity among all men. The traditional peasant commune was viewed as reflective of the Slav's primordial union with freedom and social harmony. While the rightist Official Nationality policy of Nicholas I tended to conflict with the liberal notions of the Slavophiles, his disastrous involvement in the debacle of the Crimean War (1854-55) led his son, Tsar Alexander II (1855-81), to inaugurate the Era of the Great Reforms in Russia to modernize the nation and abolish the onerous state of serfdom.

91

As early as 1840, Count Paul Kiselev, as head of the Ministry of Imperial Domains, was commissioned to study the implication of a general emancipation of the serfs. His investigations led to little constructive change under Nicholas I although Kiselev's study of the rural populace revealed the conspicuous isolation of the German colonies. His findings were essentially confirmed by an earlier report by a Kontor official who related that "there are only a few of the colonists who enlighten themselves as much as they should concerning the Russian language, wherefore they do not know the Russian laws...and evidently take pains to avoid every intercourse with Russia."[1] It was realized that the contributing factor to this situation was their special status as *kolonisty* which guaranteed certain advantages not available to the general public. Accordingly, legislation altering their judicial and political systems was introduced in the 1860s. In 1861 Russia's twenty-five million serfs were freed from serfdom and in 1864 zemstvo reform established district and provincial assemblies among all classes through an indirect electoral process and within a decade these were functioning in the Volga, uniting both Germans and Russians in common assemblies. Local colonial autonomy was now replaced by the integrated zemstvos which had jurisdiction over education, public finances, and other matters.

Since in most areas of colonial settlement the Germans remained the predominant ethnic group, they generally acquiesced to these changes. It was not until 1871 that these developments culminated in a decree perceived by thousands of Volga Germans as unacceptably minacious. By that time the flourishing colonies also attracted an element of suspicion due to their comparative prosperity. "One hundred years after Catherine had called the Germans to the Volga, they had progressed to a level of farming leadership in Russia. Their farms were models of productivity to all the native Russians."[2]

The Ukase of June 4, 1871 was promulgated by the Council of Ministers just as routinely as other policies of the day. It was to have, however, far-reaching effects on the Germans in Russia. The senate decree repealed all privileges originally granted "for eternal time" under the terms of Catherine's 1763 Manifesto including military exemption. Attempts by a sympathetic tsar and his foreign minister, Prince Alexander Gorchakov, to modify the military exemption clause succeeded only in allowing a ten-year grace period in which colonists would have the option to legally emigrate although few of these landed people seemed eager to do so. Grievances expressed to the authorities brought no redress and even Alexander II remarked with reference to the sudden abrogation that "a hundred years is an eternity!"[3]

The temporary exemption did, however, serve to quell domestic agitation among the Germans, who had never exhibited violent political temperament. Furthermore, the most significant changes in the law involved their administrative and legal status, issues that were typically remote to the isolated colonists. In terms of their status, the term *kolonist* was replaced with *poselianin-sobstvennik* (settler-owner) which denoted a "foreign rural resident who owned land and who was legally equal to rural residents of Russian nationality *(selskeya-obitatelye)*."[4] Other changes in terminology mandated to the Russian such terms as *selo* (village), *volost* (a group of villages), *uyezd* (several *volosti)* and *gubernia* (province). While German officials generally continued now as village elder *(sel'skii starotsa)* and volost elder *(volostnoi starshina),* their records now had to be kept in Russian and control at the upper levels of government jurisdiction shifted away from the German minority.[5] The Russians now dominated the civil administration of the region since the Saratov *Kontor* of the Guardianship Committee was also abolished in 1871, the affairs of these former colonies now assigned to the Ministry of the Interior.

A decisive preemption of the ordered transition toward assimilation with the Russian populace occurred with the unexpectedly early issuance of the law of universal military conscription and corresponding annulment of the grace period on January 1, 1874. The dread of serving in the Russian army was widespread among the males in the nation and especially the Germans, many of whom had a poor command of the Russian language and were often looked upon with disdain in the predominantly native Russian regiments. Discipline was cruel with minimum chance for advancement and terms of service lasted up to six years. Wages were pitifully low and the eligible draft age began at twenty. Lotteries were held to fill the ranks of the standing army.[6] The threat of conscription became the chief motivating factor for the initial emigration of Germans from Russia to North and South America and in 1874 over 6,000 Germans, predominately Mennonites, immigrated to the United States. A tragic drought struck the Volga region in 1878 along with cattle diseases as well as epidemics of typhus and smallpox among the people. The resulting economic decline prompted continued German emigration from Russia as did events during the reactionary reigns of Alexander II (1881-94) and Nicholas II (1894-1917).[7]

Large scale German emigration from Russia to the Americas at this time began in the Black Sea region in response to favorable reports communicated by some of their number who had located in the Midwest as early as 1849.[8] The encouraging news of opportunity abroad coupled with their growing political consternation led a group of twenty-one families from Johannestal, Worms, and Rohrbach to emigrate in the fall of 1872, most settling in Ohio and the Territory of Dakota near Yankton. Some Mennonite colonists from the Black Sea region also sought refuge elsewhere at this time as the military terms of the 1871 Ukase were in conflict with their religious beliefs. In 1872 a group petitioned the American consulate in Odessa requesting the position of the United States government regarding the possibilities of their special settlement in that country. The consul advised them favorably, indicating that not only would their religious views be respected but that the Northern Pacific Railroad and others could assist them in finding desirable lands to purchase as well as offer reduced transportation rates and temporary employment on line construction. In the summer of 1873, a delegation of twelve Mennonite "elders" was sent to explore areas of Canada and the United States and an exodus began the following year.[9]

Although the Volga Germans were generally more

94

secluded from the political affairs of the nation, they too became alarmed at the trend toward Russification as evidenced by repeal of the original Manifesto and subsequent legislation. In addition, antagonism was still being directed against the pietistic Brethren in many Volga colonies. By contrast, there was strong attraction to North America brought about by the early immigrants to the United States who reported to their friends and relatives in the Old World about the many opportunities of the New World. Promotional literature was sent to Europe expounding upon the wealth of the country and the rich soil that was yet to be turned.

In the spring of 1874, mass meetings were held to discuss the situation among Catholic colonists on the *Wiesenseite* at Herzog and in Balzer on the *Bergseite* by the Protestants. A prime mover in the drive to emigrate was Rev. Wilhelm Stärkel, the Reformed pastor in Norka who, having done mission work in Kansas and Missouri in the 1860s, extolled the virtues of that land and related the liberal provisions of the Homestead Act of 1862.[10] Accordingly, a total of fourteen scouts were selected to explore potential areas of settlement in the United States. Sailing from Hamburg on July 1, 1874 on the *S. S. Shiller,* the *Kundschafter* included:[11]

(Catholic)
> Peter Leiker, Obermonjour
> Jacob Ritter, Luzern
> Nicholas Schamne, Graf
> Peter Stöklein, Zug
> Anton Wasinger, Schönchen
> Anton Käberlein, Pfeifer

(Protestant)
> Johannes Krieger, Norka
> Johannes Nolde, Norka
> Georg Kähm, Balzer
> Heinrich Schwabauer, Balzer
> Christoph Meisinger, Messer
> Johann Benzel, Kolb
> Franz Scheibel, Kolb
> Georg Stieben, (unknown)

Upon arrival in the United States, the party divided into several units to explore areas in Nebraska, Kansas, Iowa, and possibly Arkansas, Prairie grass and a soil sample were retrieved to confirm their optimistic report upon their return to the Volga as was technical information regarding the various modes of transportation and settlement. In the fall and winter of 1874, a small group departed for Nebraska, Kansas, and Arkansas. One year later, on August 23, 1875 emigrants from Balzer, Dietel, and Mohr went to Red Oak, Iowa under the leadership of Heinrich Schwabauer. Part of this group followed Jacob Bender to Sutton, Nebraska where they had heard Black Sea Germans had settled, while others went to Kansas. In November of that same year, Catholics from the Volga reached Topeka and Rush County, Kansas. Both Topeka and Lincoln became central distribution points for Volga German settlement in the region which began *en mass* in the summer of 1876.[12] A number of Protestant families arriving that year formed the basis of two separate groups that would almost simultaneously leave Kansas and Nebraska for the Pacific Northwest.

During these years many Germans in Russia were also induced to explore settlement possibilities in Brazil, Argentina, and Canada. Large scale immigration to South America began in 1877, while in western Canada the lack of railroad service and the colder climate delayed significant immigration there until after 1896. Nevertheless the movement of Russian Germans to the Americas grew to massive proportions in the period from 1874 to 1914. The flood of immigration from Europe in general was interrupted after 1914 as a result of World War I. Prior to the war's outbreak, however, approximately 300,000 Russian Germans immigrated to the Americas as their plight in Russia went from bad to worse.

Following the assassination of the reforming Tsar Alexander II in 1881, his reactionary son, Alexander III (1881-94), countered in a reign characterized by further attempts directed, in the words of Peter Durnovo, chief of the state police, "toward the complete liberation of Russia from the foreign element."[13] Such sentiment at higher levels of government led to anti-German policy in both the foreign and domestic realm, continued under Nicholas I (1894-1917). A ukase issued on March 26, 1892, prohibited the private ownership of land by foreign residents in Russia — the status of the Volga Germans — and forbade the leasing of land by foreigners. Immunity from these stipulations was contingent upon application for naturalization and membership in the Russian Orthodox Church, an unlikely prospect to most Volga Germans.[14]

Their school systems also came increasingly under the scrutiny of the authorities and in 1890 legislation was introduced requiring a Russian teacher in every German school, followed by a decree in 1897 requiring Russian as the principal language of instruction. In 1905 certain restrictions on the private ownership of land and use of German were rescinded, but the status of German ethnicity in Russia continued to be precarious. Finally, per capita land supply continued to regress with the growing population while tragic crop failures struck the Volga region in 1884, 1889, 1892, and 1897.[15] The developments continued in great contrast to revelations of prosperity and security in America.

In some respects, Russia and the United States were undergoing similar changes in the late nineteenth century. Both were becoming more aware of their great natural wealth and had recently met the problems of servile emancipation while looking forward to growth in transportation and industry. Relations between the two countries were good and while William F. Cody supervised a spirited buffalo hunt on Grand Duke Alexis' United States tour in 1872, both nations' diplomats often referred to mutual "manifest destinies." However, the United States, though not always oblivious to ethnic distinctions, molded a new order in the nineteenth century through unprecedented achievements in transportation, agriculture, and education.[16] Revision of the Homestead Act of 1862 led to grants of available land to foreigners who simply declared their intentions of becoming United States citizens through which they could secure a deed to a 160 acre tract after having cultivated a portion of it for five years. Preemptions could be obtained under the same qualifications but after only six months of residence at $1.25 per acre. Supplementary federal legislation such as the Timber Culture Act of 1873 and Desert Land Act of 1877 eventually succeeded in filling what Abraham Lincoln had earlier termed a labor deficiency in agriculture.[17]

The completion of the first transcontinental railroad in May, 1869 was another event that sparked a new era of settlement in the American West. Not only were new areas now made readily accessible to settlers, but the scheme to subsidize the construction of over 1,000 miles of Union Pacific track was to grant lands adjacent to the lines, the sale of which would then become a profitable enterprise for the railroad. Through this arrangement Congress mandated grants totalling millions of acres to the Union Pacific as well as other railroad companies operating lines west of the Mississippi River. By 1872 the Kansas Pacific and the Atchison, Topeka and Santa Fe were given the claim to seven million acres in Kansas Territory alone, consisting of alternate sections along the right of way for twenty miles on both sides.

Carl B. Schmidt, a native of Saxony who had settled in Lawrence, Kansas was selected in 1873 to head the immigration office of the Atchison, Topeka and Santa Fe. His contacts with German ethnic groups throughout the country led him to seek communication with dissatisfied Germans in Russia in order to arrange their settlement in America. He supervised the inspection of property near Great Bend, Kansas by leaders of a contingent of Volga Germans, mostly Catholics from the *Wiesenseite,* who arrived in Baltimore on the *S.S. Ohio* on November 23, 1875 and went to Topeka, Kansas five days later.

Most of the group under the tutelage of Schmidt deemed the price of land near Great Bend, $5 per acre, too expensive and later formed Catholic communities in Ellis County. Here they either homesteaded or purchased lands offered there for less by the Kansas Pacific Railroad with the first families arriving in Hays and Victoria in February, 1876.[18] A contemporary reporter's commentary described the scene of their arrival in the following terms:

> The whole outfit, wagons, horses, dogs, cows, women, and children of the men folks of the Russians, who had taken claims in this (Ellis) county, arrived last Wednesday night and a queer looking set they are. Most of them came fully supplied with stock, wagons, household furniture, etc....
>
> They are strong looking animals, and seem capable of any work, especially the women, who seem to perform as much menial labor as the children, which are numerous....[19]

Inman Line of Royal Mail Steamers

BETWEEN

EUROPE AND AMERICA

STEAM SEMI-WEEKLY.

Immense Reduction of Prices for Passage from all European Ports
TO NEW YORK.

THE STEAMERS OF THIS LINE ARE THE LARGEST AND FASTEST AFLOAT
AND CARRY THE BRITISH AND UNITED STATES MAIL

An Experienced Physician and Surgeon on Board.
MEDICAL TREATMENT IN CASE OF SICK-NESS, FREE OF CHARGE.

AGENTS IN EUROPE.

LIVERPOOL,	WILLIAM INMAN.
HAMBURG,	FALCK & CO.
BREMEN,	C. L. BŒDICKER.
ANTWERP,	WILLIAM INMAN.

For Passage apply to

JOHN G. DALE, NEW YORK.
or to J. F. FUNK & BRO. Elkhart. Ind

100

Subsequent statements also noted another interesting quality of Volga German life: "One of the pleasing features of the Russian presence in our town is their singing. All have good voices, and none have any hesitancy in displaying their vocal accomplishments."[20]

Among the few Protestants on board the November *S.S. Ohio* transport were the following family heads (most locating near Great Bend, Kansas): George Brach, Peter Ochs, Henry Scheuermann, and two Conrad Scheuermanns.[21] They were soon joined in Kansas by the families of George H. Green, Henry Rothe, and Conrad Aschenbrenner who had arrived in New York on January 6, 1876 on the *S.S. City of Montreal.*[22] These families began forming the nucleus from which Russian German immigration to the Pacific Northwest would be first undertaken in 1881.

Songs of lament grew in intensity on the Volga as more Germans tore the bonds of family and homeland to emigrate to America. The news of local *V'shteyeroongen* became more frequent as families auctioned off most household wares to pay travel expenses. They took little more than the physical necessities of food and clothing along with the *Wolga Gesangbuch* and family Bible which were all carefully packed in a large wooden-ribbed trunk. Travel from the Volga region was facilitated by the linking of Saratov in 1871 by railroad with southern and northern points. This also opened the region to foreign contact through visits by American railroad immigration agents with literature extolling the virtues of life in the Midwest.[23]

The general pattern of travel began upon receipt of a passport from the provincial capitals of Saratov or Pokrovsk. Since the authorities often denied requests for permanent residence abroad, some applicants registered for temporary certification while intending to flee induction into the army. Railroad service from Saratov made connections for travel to Bremen, Hamburg, or other European port cities where enormous passenger vessels transported them across the Atlantic in a normal two-week journey to Baltimore, Philadelphia, or Castle Gardens, New York. Like so many other immigrants to the United States, many Russian Germans had their first ex-

103

periences in dealing with the New World at one of these unpleasant receiving stations, particularly Castle Gardens which was the largest in all of North America prior to 1892. The principal passenger lines used by the Volga Germans included the Hamburg American Line, the Inman Line of Liverpool, and North German Lloyd (of Bremen).

Other Volga Germans who were among the first to settle in the Pacific Northwest traveled aboard the *S.S. Mosel* which arrived in New York on October 24, 1876 carrying over 200 Volga Germans largely from the *Wiesenseite* where most had lived in the daughter colonies along the Jereslan River of Neu Jagodnaja, Schöntal, Schönfeld, and Schöndorf. Villages there had been established in the 1850s principally by residents of Jagodnaja Poljana and Pobotschnoje on the *Bergseite* but unfavorable conditions along the Jereslan prompted another move. Having brethren who had settled in Kansas in 1875 (those noted previously on the *S.S. Ohio* and *S.S. City of Montreal)*, these Volga Germans also chose to emigrate and eventually formed the basis of a "Kansas colony" that would be the first group of Russian Germans to move to the Pacific Northwest. They settled in Portland, Oregon in 1881 and in Whitman County, Washington Territory the following year.[24]

Families aboard the October transport of the *S.S. Mosel* included those of Conrad Appel; Mrs. Henry Brach; Christian, John, and Phillip Kleweno; Henry Litzenberger; Conrad, Henry, Phillip, John, John Phillip, and two Peter Ochses; Adam and Henry Repp; Adam Ruhl; John, Henry, Peter, and two George and Adam Scheiermanns, and Henry Scheuermann.[25] This group traveled to Lawrence, Kansas where they stayed for about a month in the fall of 1876 while it was determined where they would settle, eventually moving to Great Bend and Pawnee Rock where some established small businesses or worked for the railroad. Most, however, selected lands to farm and many settled in areas along the border of Barton and Rush County.[26]

Intermarriage solidified relationships between the various pioneer families to form a close-knit ethnic group that would soon immigrate westward. These early pioneers of the

Northwest often lived in isolated areas where the bond of the groups of families was extremely important for their physical survival and their social well-being. This was certainly true for Henry Rothe, a native of Frank and former resident of Schönfeld on the *Wiesenseite,* who migrated to the United States with his family and settled in Bison, Kansas. Through his daughter's marriage with Phillip Green in 1878, the Rothe family formed a formal bond with the Green family. Phillip's father, George Henry Green who originally was from the Volga colony of Norka but moved to Rosenfeld, had traveled with the Rothe family to America and had settled in Otis, Kansas. Thus the two families had known each other for some time, but a strong bond was welded between the two families as a result of the marriage of Phillip and Anna Margaret. This example of a marital relationship developing into family bonds occurred often and strengthened the ethnic identity of the Volga Germans.[27] Like the Rothe and Green families, there were others who ventured to the Great Plains seeking prosperity. Mrs. Henry Brach, for example, settled with her sons near Otis where they later became prominent in business and farming. Her son Peter's wife, Sophie (Kniss) was the sister-in-law of one of the Ochs cousins, John Peter, who remained in Great Bend, Kansas with others seeking employment on the Atchison, Topeka and Santa Fe Railroad. They were all from the colony of Schönfeld. Many Volga Germans were compelled to live in old railroad cars due to their lack of finances and the lack of suitable housing in the area. One of the Schierman brothers, John, was a skilled carpenter and butcher, opening a small grocery store in Great Bend.[28] John and Anna Marie's daughter, Mary, married one of the Ochs cousins, Peter. Henry Litzenberger and Henry Repp were brothers-in-law as their wives, Anna Elizabeth and Mary (Baht) respectively, were sisters and all of these people were from Neu Jagodnaja.[29]

The Volga Germans who migrated to the Great Plains did not experience the extreme forms of discrimination that other ethnic and religious groups experienced. This was due in part to the character of the Russian Germans. Besides being recognized as a hard-working industrious people, they were known for their willingness to learn the English language and to participate in the educational opportunities of the American frontier. Many Volga Germans deemed the American system of public education superior to the educational institutions of Russia. One Kansas newspaper, the Russel *Record,* noted in 1876 that "what pleases us the best is to see them (the Russian Germans) sending their children to public school. We will risk any people's becoming Americanized, who patronize free schools." The accomplishments of the Kansas colony was equaled by those of the Nebraska colony. In Nebraska, the Volga and Black Sea Germans busied themselves with the essential elements of settlement and survival.[30]

Russian Germans who formed the Nebraska colony were eventually to become the first individuals from the Volga to settle in Adams' and Lincoln Counties of eastern Washington. Most of the Volga Germans of the Nebraska colony were from the same general area of *Bergseite,* and they moved to Nebraska because of the influence of Black Sea Germans. The Black Sea people who had settled near Sutton served to confirm for many Volga Germans that the sod in Nebraska was very productive. The Black Sea group originally consisted of fifty-five families from Worms and Rohrbach who emigrated in the summer of 1873 and were directed to Lincoln. After a brief foray to Dakota Territory that ended because of a cholera epidemic, the group returned to Nebraska and settled in the Sutton area.[31]

The Volga German scouts who had visited Nebraska in 1874 were favorably impressed and their testimony was enhanced by the extensive foreign advertising of the State Board of Immigration in Nebraska. It depicted the unbroken plains as a virtual Paradise — reminiscent of an earlier period in Volga German history. Ten thousand pamphlets in German and 21,000 maps of Nebraska were distributed among the Mennonites by Fritz Hedde, a state official. An immigrant settlement house was constructed in Sutton, Nebraska and the Union Pacific, Burlington, and Missouri Pacific Railroads spent an estimated one million dollars to entice European settlers to the state.[32] The Union Pacific had been awarded twelve million acres of land along its tracks

Fig. 26. S. S. Schiller. (The Mariners Museum and AHSGR)

Fig. 27. S. S. Wieland. (The Mariners Museum and AHSGR)

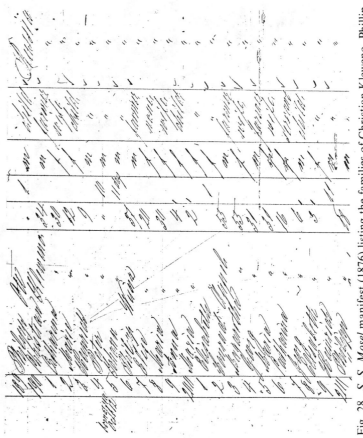

Fig. 28. *S. S. Mosel* manifest (1876) listing the families of Christian Kleweno, Phillip Wurz, and Conrad Appel. One of the Kleweno children, Johann, was born at sea. (Mrs. Emma S. Haynes)

Fig. 29. Kansas colony homestead in Rush County, 1880s. (Ramon Huntley)

Fig. 31. Mr. and Mrs. Conrad Schierman. (Mrs. Pete Konschu)

Fig. 30. Mr. and Mrs. Phillip Green. (Mrs. Richard Kaiser)

Fig. 32. The J. F. Rosenoff family. (Wayne Rosenoff)

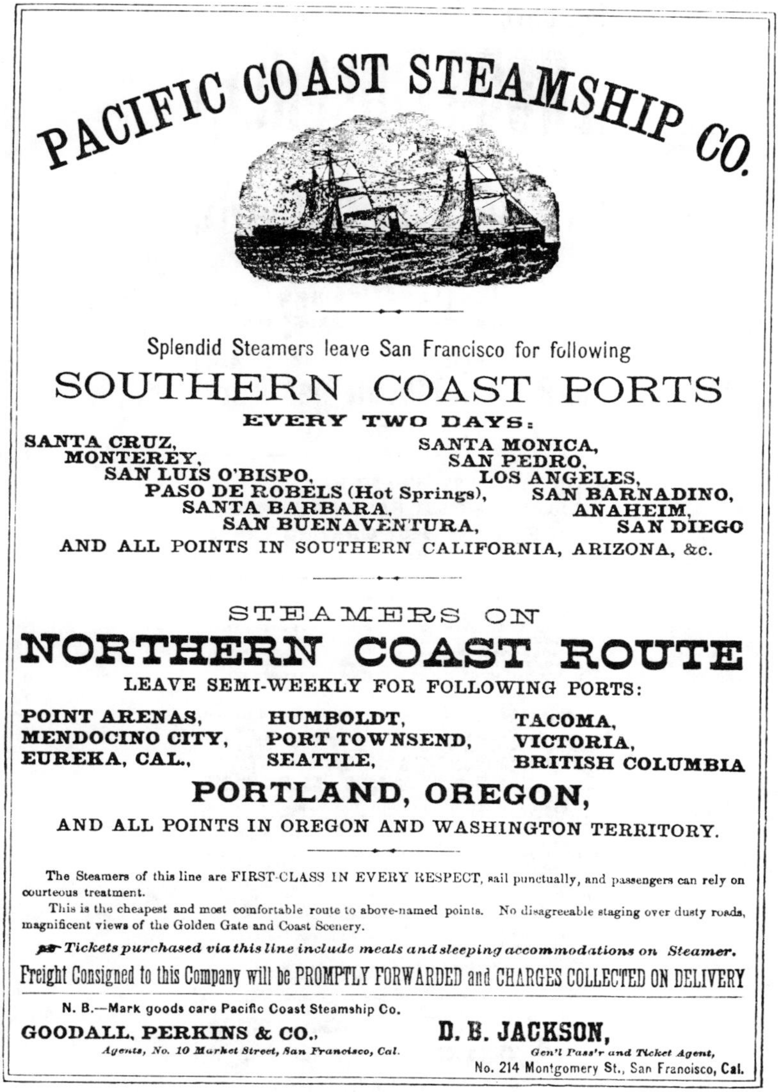

Fig. 33. Pacific Coast Steamship Advertisement.

113

NORTHERN PACIFIC RAILROAD
LANDS FOR SALE

The Northern Pacific Railroad Company Offers

OVER 36,600,000 ACRES

Of Very Productive and Desirable

Agricultural and Grazing Lands

For Sale at Prices Ranging Chiefly From

$1.25 to $10.00 per Acre

And on Five Years' Credit.

FOR THE BEST WHEAT LANDS,
FOR THE BEST FARMING LANDS,
FOR THE BEST GRAZING LANDS
IN THE WORLD.

These fertile lands are located along the line in the States traversed by the Northern Pacific Railroad as follows:

IN MINNESOTA, upwards of - - 1,250,000 Acres;
IN NORTH DAKOTA, upwards of - 6,800,000 Acres;
IN MONTANA, upwards of - - - 17,450,000 Acres;
IN NORTHERN IDAHO, upwards of - 1,750,000 Acres;
IN WASHINGTON and OREGON, over 9,375,000 Acres.

Terms of Sale of Northern Pacific Railroad Lands.

Agricultural lands of the Company, east of the Missouri River in North Dakota and Minnesota, are sold chiefly at from $4.00 to $8.00 per acre, grazing lands at from $3.00 to $4.00 per acre; and the preferred stock of the Company will be received at par in payment. When lands are purchased on five years' time, one-sixth stock or cash is required at time of purchase, and the balance in five equal annual payments, with interest at 7 per cent.

The price of Agricultural lands in North Dakota, west of the Missouri River, ranges chiefly from $2.50 to $5.00 per acre and in Montana from $3.00 to $5.00 per acre. If purchased on five years' time, one-sixth cash, and the balance in five equal annual cash payments, with interest at 7 per cent. per annum.

The price of Agricultural lands in Washington, east of the Cascade Mountains, and in Oregon and Idaho, ranges chiefly from $2.50 to $6 per acre, and in that portion of Washington west of the Cascades the price ranges chiefly from $3 to $15 per acre. If purchased on five years' time one-fifth cash. At end of first year, the interest only on the unpaid amount. One-fifth of principal and interest due at end of each of next four years. Interest at 7 per cent. per annum.

Grazing Lands west of the Missouri River in North Dakota and in Montana and Washington are sold at from $1.25 to $2.50 per acre, according to location and quality and on from one to five years' time.

Timber and Timber Lands in Minnesota and Washington are sold at prices and on terms to be arranged by special agreement with the General Land Agents.

Rebate for Cultivation.—A rebate of $1.00 per acre will be deducted from last payment on lands east of the Missouri River in North Dakota and Minnesota, broken and put under cultivation within two years from date of purchase. No rebate allowed after full payment is made.

Rates of Fare.—For rates of fare for settlers and for emigrant fares and freight rates for household goods and emigrant movables, see page 5.

Notice.—The land department of the Northern Pacific Railroad Company employs no agents or others along its line who are authorized to receive or receipt for any moneys for the Company, or to bind the Company by any agreements or acts whatsoever.

All applications for the purchase of Northern Pacific Railroad Lands in Wisconsin, Minnesota, Dakota, and Montana, and all payments thereon, must be made to WILLIAM WAUGH, General Land Agent at St. Paul, Minn., and all applications for the purchase of the Company's lands in Washington, Idaho, and Oregon, and all payments thereon, must be made to PAUL SCHULZE, General Land Agent, at Tacoma, Wash.

Fig. 34. "Lands for Sale," Northern Pacific Railroad.

from Omaha to Promontory Point, Utah and together with other railroads, it opened vast areas in Nebraska for sale and development.[33]

Booming grain production in the Midwest contributed to a 100% increase in the export of farm commodities from the United States between 1871 and 1874. This agricultural development was brought about by the advancement of American technology, and these new changes severely reduced Russia's traditional hold on the European market because its production declined during the same period.[34] Many Germans from Russia first settled in the Midwest where agriculture was rapidly becoming an important national source of wealth and pride. Indeed, the word "bunchgrass" became synonomous with untapped soil fertility in America's Midwest, and one published account by a trading firm in Odessa, Russia ventured to suggest a significant development resulting from the expansion of American agriculture: "The mind is positively lost in painful thought when considering the quantity of corn (grain) America will soon be able to export. America will absolutely command the English market, and reduce prices to a minimum, with which it will be utterly impossible for us to compete."[35]

In 1875 a number of Volga German families from Balzer settled near Sutton after an unfavorable reception in Iowa. They were joined the following year by a number of families from Norka.[36] On August 5, 1876 the *S.S. Donau* docked in New York carrying a large number of Volga Germans who had departed Kolb and Dietel on June 25. Among the Kolb group were several families who would later compose a portion of the Nebraska colony that moved to Washington Territory in 1882. Among the families who arrived on the *S.S. Donau* in 1876, were Henry Bauer, Henry Kanzler, Henry Rehn, and Franz Scheibel, a member of the earlier scouting party who had been the schoolteacher in Kolb.[37] Scheibel and his group endured a difficult circuitous journey to Nebraska, directed at first to Dorchester in Clark County, Wisconsin. The forested terrain was hardly suited for farming, and after several days, during which the Henry Bauer infant died, it was decided to seek a more promising site in Nebraska. When they reached Chicago, they were given employment as laborers for the Burlington Railroad which arranged for their free passage to Hastings, Nebraska. Accordingly, the party arrived there in August, 1876. After a week, some members of the group were induced to purchase lands in Franklin County, southwest of Hastings; their transportation again furnished by the railroad. They wintered in a settlement house on the Little Blue River and later established St. Paul's Church under Scheibel in the small village of Wilhelmsruhe.[38]

For several years the Volga German settlers farmed there, living in sod houses and marketing their grain in nearby Hastings. The group was joined by a number of families in 1878 from villages on the *Bergseite* who arrived on June 5 in New York on the *S.S. Wieland*. Many passengers on this voyage were from Kolb, and they formed the other major segment of the Nebraska colony: The families of J. Frederick Rosenoff and Jacob Thiel with his sons George and John and their families and, from Frank, the Conrad Kiehns and Henry Amen, both of whom had immigrated with their parents. Other families on the same trip included Heim-bigners, (Norka and Frank), Schösslers (Walter), Hoffs (Frank), Müllers (Kolb), Dewalds (Hussenbach), and others.[39]

It was decided in 1878 that prospects for expansion would be greater for the colony in the southwest portion of the state despite the climate which in that area was semiarid.[40] Nevertheless, in September they filed on homesteads in Hitchcock County near Culbertson, Nebraska and moved in May, living in soddies along Blackwood Creek. They made their livelihood by raising livestock and harvesting crops there as well as on their acreage in Franklin County. Large gardens provided the settlers with a variety of vegetables and melons while wild fruits grew abundantly along the river.[41] Unfortunately their contentment was again shortlived in as much as they soon learned that their settlement was located near the Western Cattle Trail, a major thoroughfare for the long drives of Texas Longhorns to the northern markets. Their fields and gardens were overrun by cattle and their miseries were compounded by a disastrous drought on the Great Plains during the early 1880s. This led many to consider moving to a region which would become their ultimate destination. The same move was being contemplated simultaneously by members of the Kansas colony. Both groups were looking toward America's northern frontier — the Pacific Northwest.

The Kansas colony suffered considerably from the effects of the grasshopper plagues in the late 1870s. Particularly from 1875 to 1877, massive hordes of these insects so infested the fields and air that the Germans were left with little seed to replant. A dismal gloom hung over the land as swarms of the pests darkened the midday sky. The subsequent drought also adversely affected them and some remarked of the terror felt during the frightening electrical storms. The Germans were not accustomed to such storms in Russia, and they dreaded the devastation of the plains tornados.[42] One informant humorously related an Oz-like fantasy in which a cyclone was said to have taken a small lake and team of horses from a Rush County homestead which his father, after he came out of the root cellar, attempted to find. Enroute to town he found the road leading into a new lake and nearby the two horses stood — still harnessed and unharmed![43]

Because of these conditions on the plains, many disgruntled immigrant groups in the Midwest increasingly considered the possibility of settling in the Pacific Northwest. The settlers learned from some men who had worked in the Oregon Country on railway surveys that the land was fertile and beautiful. Their interest was further stimulated by the favorable descriptions provided by transportation companies from the Pacific Northwest. In order to encourage emmigration, these companies advertised the lush regions of the inland Northwest as the "Great Columbia Plain." Not only were transportation companies that owned land interested in selling acreage, but they also wanted to tap an unskilled labor source for the construction of their railroads. In order to fill this need, company officials turned to immigrants for a solution. Various railroad companies formed associations offering reduced rates to those who would travel westward to settle while guaranteeing employment until such arrangements were possible. The Union Pacific, Northern Pacific, Oregon Steamship Company, and others were particularly interested in encouraging the development of the West in order to profit not only from passenger service but the anticipated shipment of industrial and agricultural commodities that were to be developed by the transportation companies.

One man's name in particular became synonomous with the growth and development of the Northwest — Henry Villard — who by 1876 had shrewdly wrested control of Northwestern transportation systems from railroad magnate Ben Holladay of Overland Stage and Pony Express fame. In the centennial year, Villard assumed the presidency of several companies that were heavily in debt, including the Oregon and California Railroad and the Oregon Central Railroad, both of which were far from completion. In addition, Villard gained control of the Oregon Steamship Company which operated regularly between San Francisco and Portland.[44] Within six years Henry Villard's position in Northwest transportation was clearly paramount as his holdings appeared secure and were among the largest of any individual in the entire nation. It was through the instrumentality of Villard's companies, principally the Oregon Railway and Navigation Company and the Northern Pacific Railroad, that the first Volga Germans settled in the Pacific Northwest.

4

SETTLEMENT IN THE PACIFIC NORTHWEST

Wenn wir auf dem Wasser
fahren,
Schickt uns Gott einen Engel
dar,
Gott, streck aus deine milde
Hand,
Dass wir kommen an das Land.
When we upon the water sail,
God sends an angel without
fail.
Stretch out then, God, Thy
gentle hand,
That we can safely come on
land!
    —"Auswandererlied," v. 5

The ultimate fate of many Volga Germans was linked very closely to the life of Henry Villard, a native of Speyer. He came to the United States in 1853 and labored for several years in various occupations. Well educated in Germany, he studied law in Carlisle, Illinois and worked in the offices of several influential United States senators from the Midwest. Finding a talent in journalism, he reported on various political campaigns for several newspapers, and he was on hand to cover the Lincoln-Douglas debates in 1859. His experiences led to personal acquaintanceships with Abraham Lincoln, Horace Greeley, and other people in influential circles of American business and politics. He became increasingly interested in the subject of railroad securities and finance, although for reasons of health he was compelled to return to Germany for recuperation in 1870 and again in 1871. He remained in Germany until 1873.

His growing reputation in American journalism combined with his coverage of the European Prussian wars enabled him to establish many business contacts on the continent. This was a significant development because of the business link it would provide him in the future as he promoted economic growth in the Pacific Northwest. Villard was keenly aware that several European finance houses, chiefly the firm of Sulzbach Brothers, had invested heavily in Ben Holladay's Oregon and California Railroad bonds, the value of which were steadily declining. The young entrepreneur hoped to use his business associates to develop the economic potentials of the American West. Aware of Villard's experience in America and his expertise in economic and political matters, he was approached in 1873, while convalescing in Heidelberg, to advise a protective committee based in Frankfurt. After several discussions on the matter, Villard was invited to join the committee which he formally did in the spring of 1873. The chief problem, however, remained a lack of detailed information about the committee's investments on the distant Pacific Coast of North America. To correct the problem, the committee sent an inspection team to Oregon in April which soon returned to Germany with a very discouraging report.[1]

Due to Villard's proficiency in English, he and Richard Köhler were appointed to proceed with others to the United States in order to execute a financial settlement with Holladay's troubled enterprise. Departing in April of 1874, Villard first attended a meeting in New York with Holladay which provided the German an opportunity to comment on Holladay's "illiteracy, coarseness, presumption, mendacity, and unscrupulousness."[2] These impressions would lead to an intense rivalry between the two. Villard was not satisfied with the interview with Holladay and decided to see for himself the conditions in the Pacific Northwest. He set out for Oregon in May of 1874 arriving in San Francisco in June. There Villard and his associates boarded the California and Oregon Railroad and traveled by alternate rail and wagon route to Portland.

Villard was awed by the scenery of the Pacific Coast and

the Willamette Valley. He reported that "the beautiful land-scapes unrolled to us one after another and framed the east by the green clad Cascades, overtopped by its isolated snow-covered peaks, and to the west by the picturesque Coast Range." Moreover, he was impressed, too, with the evidence of agricultural wealth in the broad wheat fields that greeted the eye." Villard felt that he "had reached a chosen land, certain of great prosperity and seemingly holding out better promise to my constituents than I had hoped for."[3]

The talented entrepreneur became thoroughly imbued with a determination to capitalize on the great potentials of the region. Realizing that settlers would be needed to transform the virgin lands into acres of productivity, Villard began efforts to promote immigration to Oregon in November, 1874. Supplied with the distinction of "Oregon Commissioner of Immigration," he opened an office in the heart of Boston's financial district and named it the "Eastern Bureau of the Oregon State Board of Immigration."[4] In the following year, he established agencies in Omaha and Topeka that cooperated with the main Northwest Immigration Bureau in Portland. The major purpose of these agencies was to encourage emigrants to settle in the Pacific Northwest by offering them reduced travel rates over the lines of the Union Pacific Railroad and the Oregon Steamship Company. It was the duty of railroad officials in the Northwest to provide them with employment on construction crews or sell them land to develop.

Both of these schemes led to the further development and use of the railroads. Both made sound economic sense, for the immigrants would use the railroad to ship their livestock and grain. The immigration bureaus used various methods to promote migration to the region. Special displays were circulated of Oregon grains, fruits, and vegetables; large format advertisements appeared regularly in English, Scandinavian, and German language newspapers throughout the country; thousands of circulars and pamphlets were distributed. All of these were used as promotional materials to foster an interest in settlement of the Pacific Northwest.

Villard observed that geographically the central artery of

transportation throughout the entire Pacific Northwest was the Columbia River. He assumed that whoever navigated the great stream and controlled the railways along its course virtually monopolized transportation east of the Cascades. He would embark on a grand scheme of uniting both water and rail routes and placing these under his personal control. Although traveling extensively in both the United States and Europe, he skillfully managed the affairs of the European financiers whom he represented while formulating his plans.

He journeyed up the Columbia to The Dalles for the first time in May 1876.[5] Impressed by the great natural beauty of the area and imposing basaltic formations, he noted the natural outlet of the vast fertile and untouched regions drained by the Columbia and Snake Rivers, the control of which "influenced my thoughts with enticing visions of the empire that could be built upon such resources and of the share I might secure in founding and developing it." According to Villard, "it was at that early date that a plan arose distinctly in my mind which remained ever present with me until it was carried out through the organization of the Oregon Railway and Navigation Company."[6]

Within a year Villard's manipulation of several heavily indebted concerns led him to the presidency of three companies: the Oregon and California Railroad, the Oregon Central Railroad, and the Oregon Steamship Company, the latter of which operated a regular schedule between San Francisco and Portland.[7] An important component in the migration of immigrants to the Pacific Northwest was the northern transcontinental railroad. President Lincoln had signed the Northern Pacific Act on July 4, 1864, but construction was delayed because of the Civil War. Extensive land grants amounting to 25,000 acres of adjacent land per mile of track[8] had been granted to the company to encourage construction, but no progress was made until the summer of 1870 when work commenced at Thompson Junction Mission on Lake Superior in Minnesota. On the Pacific side, grading began at Kalama, Washington Territory north up the Cowlitz Valley toward Puget Sound in December of the same year. However, the financial panic of 1873 led to the bankruptcy of the Northern Pacific Railroad company in 1875, and the Northern Pacific lost control of the Oregon Steam Navigation Company, the integral link in the system between Ainsworth and Portland. Villard realized this was a major opportunity to gain a foothold in the transcontinental traffic and subsequently purchased the Oregon Steam Navigation Company with their portage roads at the Cascades, The Dalles, and Celilo Falls. With the election of the energetic Frederick Billings to the presidency of the Northern Pacific Railroad in 1879, work was resumed at both ends of the beleaguered line and the prospects of final completion brightened.

Materials were needed on the construction of the Northern Pacific's Pend Oreille division which stretched from Ainsworth, Washington northeasterly through Spokane to Lake Pend Oreille. It was a massive undertaking employing thousands and provided a strong local market for agricultural produce. Villard was now in the position to provide the needed supply services through his river route. Accordingly, he entered into traffic agreements in 1880 with Billings through which Villard's Oregon Railway and Navigation Company carried materials to Ainsworth while contracting to build a line down the left bank of the Columbia River with feeder lines extending into eastern Oregon and Washington Territory. For this purpose he had organized with eastern capital the Oregon Railway and Navigation Company in June, 1879 which assumed control of the Oregon Steam Navigation Company and the Oregon Steamship Company. After the purchase of Dr. D. S. Baker's narrow gauge line from Wallula[9] to Walla Walla, Villard gained complete control of transportation from Wallula to Portland and from there by steamer to San Francisco.[10]

The agreement reached with the Northern Pacific further stipulated a division of interest between the two lines with the Columbia and Snake Rivers forming the boundary line. An exception was made in deference to Villard's insistence on a detached Palouse line, construction of which was being planned from Palouse Junction (Connell) eastward through the heart of the fertile Palouse Hills to Endicott and Colfax, leading eventually to the Coeur d'Alene mining district. It was in this central Palouse region that many Volga Germans were led to settle.

Improvements in transportation and agricultural mechanization led to increased agricultural production east of the Cascades. Only half of the crop of 1879 could be exported before navigation of the rivers ended in December for the winter.[11] Transportation however, was not completely halted, for up to 1800 settlers were moving to the Columbia Plain each month. They came by wagon up the south bank of the Columbia enroute to fertile lands in the Walla Walla area, Big Bend country, and the Palouse Hills.[12]

To facilitate the orderly settlement and exploitation of their holdings in this region, Villard incorporated the Oregon Improvement Company on October 21, 1880 with capital stock of $5,000,000 provided by American financial associates. The Oregon Improvement Company purchased the Seattle Coal and Transportation Company and the Seattle and Walla Walla Railroad, the forerunner of the Pacific Coast Railway. In addition to other land acquisition, the new company bought nearly 150,000 acres (alternate sections in fourteen townships) from the Northern Pacific in the heart of the Palouse country, these being carefully selected and varying in price from $5 to $10 per acre, selling on a six year installment plan at 7% interest.[13] Many of the early Volga German arrivals in the area, however, found that land was more easy to obtain by homesteading.

Villard appointed General Thomas R. Tannatt of Manchester, Massachusetts to handle the affairs of the Oregon Improvement Company. Tannatt was a prominent New England figure and retired brigadier general who had commanded Union forces south of the Potomac in 1862. During his command in defense of the capitol, he became personally acquainted with President Lincoln. He was later reassigned to the Second Army Corps. In 1864 he was severely wounded in action at Petersburg. For reasons of health he moved to Colorado after the Civil War where he managed the mining interests of several New York investors before relocating to McMinnville, Tennessee in 1870. In 1876 he

Fig. 35. Henry Villard. (Minnesota Historical Society)

Fig. 36. Thomas R. Tannatt (Washington State University Libraries)

Fig. 37. Northern Pacific Railroad depot in Spokane, 1883.

Fig. 38. Northern Pacific "Immigrant Train". (Luke Benner)

Fig. 39. Walla Walla, Washington Territory, c. 1880. (Washington State University Libraries)

returned to Massachusetts and became increasingly interested in developing railroad land grants in the Pacific Northwest.[14] This prompted him to write a letter to Villard in 1877 in which he offered several suggestions which would aid in the westward settlement of immigrants. Impressed with the advice, Villard appointed him the eastern agent for the Oregon Steamship Company in 1877, and in the following year he began directing the immigration program for Villard's other Northwest transportation companies.

After the formation of the Oregon Improvement Company in 1878, Villard elevated Tannatt as its general agent and his office was transferred to Portland. S. G. Reed of that city was the Oregon Improvement Company's first president and the other directors were William Endicott, Jr., Boston; George M. Pullman, Chicago; Artemas Holmes, New York; and C. H. Lewis, Henry Failing, C. J. Smith, J. N. Dolf and C. H. Prescott, all of Portland.[15] Tannatt embarked on his new responsibilities with a vigor that characterized his entire career. He was instrumental in persuading the Oregon railroads and the Oregon Steam Navigation Company to issue reduced travel certificates to immigrants and he personally supervised the settlement of numerous immigrant groups from New England and the Midwest. He cooperated with Union Pacific ticket agencies throughout the East in order to arrange transportation to the Northwest where an intensive campaign was under way to popularize settlement in the Inland Empire. In 1882 Villard's Northern Pacific Railroad employed over 900 agents in Europe who distributed thousands of pamphlets in several languages extolling the Pacific Northwest[16] as the "best wheat, farming and grazing lands in the world."

Unknown even to his closest associates at this time, the implications of Villard's ambitious plans of railroad ownership were not only regional but national in scope.[17] He came to the realization that direct railway connections to the East were imperative if the Pacific Northwest was ever to be actively involved in the commerce of the nation and the influx of European immigrants. With this in mind, he embarked in December, 1880 on the unprecedented scheme of secretly collecting $8,000,000 from his financial supporters which formed the famous "blind pool". Reflecting their confidence in Villard, his request was actually oversubscribed, enabling him to purchase the controlling interest in Billings' Northern Pacific Railroad, work on which had again been stalemated. With Villard's election to its presidency on September 15, 1881 and work on both ends resumed, his dream of a northern transcontinental rapidly approached reality.

Work on the Oregon Railway and Navigation Company line from Portland to Wallula continued at brisk pace and although the earlier agreement with Billings specified its completion by October 31, 1883 the energetic crews of the company finished it on October 20, 1882 with the first through passenger train leaving Portland on November 20, 1882.[18] By July of that year a number of branch lines had begun fanning out in the Walla Walla country, one extending north from Walla Walla to the Snake River at Texas Ferry and the Columbia and Palouse, incorporated in 1883 by Villard, continued construction eastward from Palouse Junction to Endicott.

The program launched by Villard and Tannatt to induce settlement east of the Cascades bore fruit among many immigrants in the Midwest, including the Volga Germans. In the case of the Kansas colony in Rush and Barton Counties and the Nebraska colony in Hitchcock County, frustration was particularly evident for reasons enumerated previously. In both places a segment of these groups elected to emigrate, the former in 1881 and the latter in 1882 (See Table I). The Kansas party took advantage of reduced fares over the Union Pacific line and traveled to San Francisco where steamers of Villard's Oregon Steamship Company transported them to Portland.[19] In Portland some of the immigrants labored on the construction of the huge Albina fill while others worked at a local lumber mill.[20]

Their intention to settle on prime farmland remained foremost in their minds, however, and finding the surrounding forested areas unsuitable for this purpose, they were directed to officials of the Portland Oregon Improvement Company office to explore the possibilities of

TABLE I: KANSAS AND NEBRASKA COLONY FAMILIES IMMIGRATING TO THE PACIFIC NORTHWEST IN 1881 AND 1882.

KANSAS COLONY

Family	Mother Colony	Daughter Colony to which relocated
Conrad Appel	Jagodnaja Poljana	Schöntal (?)
Phillip Aschenbrenner	Norka	Brunnental
Phillip Fuchs	Jagodnaja Poljana	Schöntal (?)
George H. Green	Norka	Rosenfeld
John Helm	Jagodnaja Poljana	Schöntal (?)
John Kleweno	Jagodnaja Poljana	Schöntal
Phillip Kleweno	Jagodnaja Poljana	Schöntal
Henry Litzenberger	Jagodnaja Poljana	Neu Jagodnaja
Henry Ochs	Pobotschnoje	Schönfeld
Peter Ochs	Pobotschnoje	Schönfeld
John Peter Ochs	Pobotschnoje	Schönfeld
Henry (& Anna) Repp	Jagodnaja Poljana	Schöntal
Adam Ruhl	Jagodnaja Poljana	Schöntal (?)
Conrad Schierman	Jagodnaja Poljana	Schöntal (?)
Henry Schierman	Jagodnaja Poljana	Schöntal (?)
John Schierman	Jagodnaja Poljana	Schöntal (?)
George Schierman	Jagadnaja Poljana	Schöntal (?)

NEBRASKA COLONY

Family	Mother Colony
John G. Adler	Kolb
Henry Amen, Sr.	Frank
Jacob Bastrom	Frank
Mrs. Hoelfrich Bauer, Sr.	Kolb
George Jacob Dewald	Hussenbach
Phillip Gottwig (?)	Walter
Conrad Heimbigner	Frank
Henry Kanzler, Sr.	Kolb
John F. Kembel	Kolb
Conrad Kiehn	Frank
John H. Koch	Kolb
Henry F. Michel	Messer
Henry Miller	Kolb
John C. Oestreich	Messer
Henry H. Rehn (?)	Frank
Frederick Rosenoff	Kolb
Jacob Schaefer	Frank
Jacob Schoessler	Walter
Jacob Thiel, Sr.	Kolb
Jacob Wagner	Frank
Conrad Wolsborn	Frank

This listing includes only heads of families although many had married sons with children of their own. See Roy Oestreich and Evelyn Reich files for individual family members.

settlement east of the Cascades. Having just completed the purchase from the Northern Pacific of the odd sections in fourteen townships in the Palouse country totalling 150,000 acres, a scouting party was selected to view the area. Both Phillip Green and Peter Ochs were fluent in English, and thus they were selected to go with others on the tour. The Walla Walla *Weekly Statesman* noted their activities through a letter of May 11, 1881 received from Agent R. W. Mitchell of the Oregon Improvement Company's Colfax Office of the Land Department:

> Five locating agents of the Kansas colony, composed of about 70 families, passed through here Thursday on their way to inspect lands of the Oregon Improvement Company. Col. Tustin is in charge of the party. They look like solid, progressive farmers, such as we are willing to welcome to our broad acres. One of them remarked, "If the land is anything like what we've seen around Dayton, I guess we can be suited. We are surprised and delighted at what we have seen." Mr. Mitchell of the Oregon Improvement Company will meet this party in the Palouse Country next week.[21]

Writing from Dayton to Villard's office, Tannatt relayed his intentions for dealing with the group in a note on May 10. Tannatt wanted "to sell them a township and will on Mr. Oakes' return if there is any trade with them."[22] Indeed, the vanguard returned favorably impressed with the area, and Tannatt planned to meet them in Portland in order to arrange the sale.[23] However, he found them reluctant to enter into such a massive bargain on behalf of the others in Kansas without consulting them first. The negotiations took time, and it was not until the fall of 1882 that members of this Portland group moved on company lands in Whitman County. Having endured the struggle of a journey half-way around the globe to this remote area, they soon discovered brethren here who had also come from the Volga. A contingent of the Nebraska colony had decided to relocate, and they also arrived in Washington in 1882.

Some Volga Germans of the Nebraska colony had considered moving to the Pacific Northwest as early as 1880. In that year the Nebraska group at Culbertson wrote J. E. Shepherd, the immigration agent of the Oregon Railway and Navigation Company in San Francisco, expressing their interest. The letter was forwarded to Villard himself who must have been pleased to see that many immigrants could be lured to the Pacific Northwest. In the letter the farmers indicated their discontent with conditions in the Midwest. The Volga Germans wrote the company to inquire "about the country of Washington Territory." They explained that they were one hundred and sixty families strong and that their major reason for seeking a new home was "that the wheat crop has failed here for three years past." The immigrants feared another drought was imminent because of so little rain for months. Their cattle were in a deplorable condition because of the lack of range. In addition, they lived on the "open prairies" where "the heavy winds that prevail here are unendurable." The Volga Germans further stated that:

> Our houses consist of "Dug outs" and "Sod houses." Our people are all discouraged and homesick, but too far to go back to Russia, and we want to see...the Territory we have heard so much of its great yielding wheat fields and wonderful Fruit Country. We understand the Navigation Company has Rail Road land for sale. There are 160 families here, and 70 families in Clay Co. this state, and 100 families coming from Russia this Fall. I think we can locate 230 families there this fall and winter. We are desirous of seeing this country first, and our minister Mr. Kansler and myself wish to go out and see the country. And we wish to know whether you can furnish passes for two persons out and one to come back and head the colony. We are a good, honest, straightforward, hard working class of people, and the colony also instructs me to state that the *two* passes will be paid back to the Company after they are located, so as to be sure of our honesty of intention....[24]

The Volga Germans of the Nebraska colony received a favorable response from the railroad officials but it was not until 1882 that they decided to immigrate to the Pacific Northwest. In the spring of 1882, a number of these families boarded a train at North Platte, Nebraska enroute to Ogden, Utah on the Union Pacific Railroad.[25] The value of having its own direct connections to the Oregon country had become increasingly evident to the Union Pacific with the developing economy of the region. For this reason it had incorporated the Oregon Short Line in 1879 to run from Granger, Wyoming roughly along the route of the old Oregon Trail to a connection with Villard's Oregon Railroad and Navigation

Company on the Columbia at Umatilla. The line was not completed until 1884, and the enterprising men of the Nebraska colony were given temporary employment constructing this stretch of the railroad from American Falls, Idaho to Pendleton, Oregon. They first formed a train of forty wagons at Ogden and lumbered north on the California Trail until they reached the Oregon Trail near the headwaters of the Snake River.

The group chose Frederick Rosenoff to be the wagonmaster and they traveled from American Falls through Boise and Baker enroute to Walla Walla.[26] Memories of the Custer massacre of 1871 and the Bannock Indian War of 1878 were still fresh in the minds of many residents as well as the immigrants. They feared Indian attack and therefore they appointed Henry Oestreich and George H. Kanzler as scouts for the party. The Volga Germans made detailed plans for their overland journey and they proved to be a resourceful people who made do with what they had to make the trip. For example, Conrad Wolsborn, a shoemaker, did not have a pair of oxen to pull his wagon. He could not afford to purchase another animal, so he fashioned a special harness uniting both his horse and his one ox. The women were just as resourceful, for they sewed garden seeds into clothing to ensure good plantings in their new home.

The caravan encountered the usual hazards associated with pioneer travel, enduring intense heat on dusty trails which often led through areas infested with rattlesnakes. Marie Thiel, wife of John, went into confinement in Baker, giving birth to twins on April 10, 1882 only one of whom, Jacob, survived. They entrusted their earnings from work on the railroad to a former Nebraskan sheriff who accompanied them but near the end of the journey he absconded with the funds. However, they maintained a strong attachment to their cultural traditions despite the rigors of the journey. They were devout Christians and they remained steadfast in their faith, never traveling on Sundays. Instead they gathered their wagons into a large circle and held worship services each Sunday with an elder reading the lessons in German. Upon arrival in Pendleton some members of the party decided to go on to Portland although most continued north to Walla Walla. The first Volga Germans drove their wagons into Walla Walla late in the summer of 1882.[27] Because they were exhausted and the weather was changing rapidly, they decided to winter in Walla Walla while investigating the various possibilities of settlement in the region.

This was not an idle time for the Volga Germans. As the bunchgrass surrounding Walla Walla turned brown, the tired immigrants ventured out to find jobs. Some of the men found employment on farms in the area, while others contracted to haul rock for the construction of the territorial penitentiary. One of the Thiels was hired by Phillip Ritz, a successful Walla Walla farmer and businessman, to dig fence-post holes on his property near Ritzville. In addition to other extensive realities in the territory, Ritz had acquired 5,000 acres near Ritzville from the railroad in 1878. Finding that Ritz paid well for his labor, Thiel decided to continue working at Ritzville and Ritz encouraged him and his companions to settle on lands nearby.[28] Ritz was an intelligent businessman who recognized the worth of the immigrants and thus began a massive migration of Germans from Russia to Adams and Lincoln Counties.

5

REGIONAL SETTLEMENT AND EXPANSION

Wir sind ja all recht gut
emphangen,
Und können jo nichts mehr
verlangen
Wie glickich sein jo wir,
Dass wir sind alle hier,
Jetzt fallen wir auf der
Knie
und danken Gott dafuer.
We were welcomed with open
arms.
Now we're free from want
and harms.
Sorrow's turned to jubilee
We've come safe o'er the
sea.
And we fall to our knees
To praise God thankfully.
— "Die Reis' Die War Erzogen," v. 4
Translated by Nancy B. Holland

Volga German settlement in the inland Northwest took place at the beginning of a pivotal decade in regional development. Prior to the 1880s the range cattle industry had been dominant east of the Cascades since as early as the 1860s stockmen had capitalized on the vast unfenced grazing lands of the region. In the 1880s, however, their presence was challenged by the growing number of colonist farmers who were clustering in the area's fertile valleys and prairie districts.

The bitter winter of 1880-81 resulted in the financial ruin of many cattlemen with some herd losses reaching fifty per cent. Grain marketing problems had long stalled agricultural development but the completion of the Northern Pacific

Railroad in 1883 facilitated farm exports to both coastal and eastern markets. At the same time, farmers began fencing their properties with barbed wire and joining together to enact "herd laws" in order to prevent cattlemen from freely ranging their stock on the recently claimed lands.

A large region north of the Snake River in Washington formed an obvious geographic entity often called the Palouse country, and with continued settlement there it was organized in November, 1871 into Whitman County. Pioneers from the Walla Walla Valley had first settled in the Palouse along Union Flat Creek during the previous decade. In 1870, settlement began at present Colfax and Farmington and during the next two years pioneers located along Rebel Flat Creek, Pine Creek, Four Mile Creek, near present Genesee and Moscow, and at the foot of Rock Lake.[1] By 1872 the population of the area totaled about two hundred whites with this rising to about one thousand the following year.[2] In the summer of 1873, surveys began to extend the existing Territorial Road from Walla Walla to Penawawa northward to the forks of the Palouse River at Colfax and north to Spokane Falls. Other main roads intersecting the region all led from Walla Walla to Spokane and Colville country, including the Texas Road which crossed the Snake at Texas Ferry (Riparia) and the Mullan (Colville) Road which, crossing the Snake at Lyon's Ferry, paralleled the Palouse River and Cow Creek leading near the future sites of Ritzville and Sprague. A portion of this route was later followed by the Northern Pacific Railroad which greatly enhanced immigration to the area.

In 1876 a federal land office was opened in Colfax and within a year the immigration thrust began with Almota becoming the chief entry port. Additional landings were built to carry the busy ferry traffic at Penawawa and Wawawai. These sites were regularly serviced by the steamboats of the Oregon Railway and Navigation Company including the *Yakima, Nez Perces Chief, Owyhee, Tenino,* and *Spray.* By 1880 the population of Whitman County had risen to over 7,000 as settlers discovered the fertility of the Palouse loessal soils.[3]

Separated to the west of these rolling hills by the channelled scablands was the Big Bend country, a vast undulating plain lying in the Columbia crescent. As the southern part was characterized by a treeless sandy expanse, the rich loam of its northern sector was largely overlooked by settlers until the 1880s. Few individuals were more convinced than Phillip Ritz of the great agricultural potential of the region and he became enamored with the idea of its development.

Ritz accompanied representatives of the Northern Pacific on tours of the area as early as 1873, urging their commercial efforts in the region. He traveled the breadth of the nation on numerous occasions to meet with various government and railroad officials and encouraged them to promote settlement in the Big Bend.[4] At the same time he was awarded contracts by the Northern Pacific to plant maple, chestnut, locust, and other trees along its tracks from Ainsworth to Ritzville, a project Ritz embarked on as much from an experimental standpoint as financial. The Walla Walla *Statesman* optimistically predicted the results based on Ritz's earlier experience as, "those planted last year are thrifty....The experiment gave emphatic denial to the theory that the sandy soil was unproductive."[5] For his efforts, the town of Ritzville was named in his honor, platted in 1881 with other towns on that section of the Northern Pacific line.

Ritz was making great progress promoting the settlement of the plateau, and his efforts were matched by those of Tannatt. Already the Kansas colony was entering the region. According to Phillip Green, a spokesman for the Kansas colony, the Volga Germans from Kansas were rapidly approaching the Palouse country and "would be at Texas Ferry in a day or so, and asking for several four-horse teams to convey them to Plainville" which was a point between Endicott and Colfax, Washington. Green commented that the immigrants were looking forward to their new home because "the land, climate and general outlook of this country, was all that could be desired." He reported that three separate colonies from Kansas had sent inspectors to the Pacific Northwest to examine the land, and all were convinced that the region would make an excellent choice for a new home. Several of the early Volga Germans from the Kansas colony located "land for other coming immigrants" and they encouraged their families and friends to move to the inland Northwest. The response was so great that one account reported that "There is to be an exodus from Kansas this fall."[6] Members of this group were determined to locate on suitable farmland. Their previous expedition to the Palouse Hills reminded them of the terrain on the Volga *Bergseite,* and they were convinced that the Palouse had soil as rich as they had ever known. Tannatt's Oregon Improvement Company provided their fares over the Oregon Railway and Navigation Company as far as Texas Ferry where some arrived on October 17. Some of the men then walked over twenty miles to Endicott, enlisting the aid of Henry D. Smith and J. T. Person to procure wagons and returned the following day to transport the families and belongings.[7]

Carrying the pioneer necessities, the Phillip Green family traveled from Portland in a covered wagon drawn by very stubborn mules. Leaving on a warm morning late in September, they followed the Emigrant Road and soon began ascending the Cascades. On the other side of the pass it began snowing and raining with such intensity that the wagon and occupants were soon drenched. The Green's infant, Magdalena, celebrated her first birthday on October 3rd under miserable circumstances. Despite the weather, they made their way to Walla Walla. After traveling north for a time out of Walla Walla, the weary settlers finally reached their destination, on October 12, 1882. They were to build their home and a new life for themselves four miles east of Endicott, Washington Territory.[8]

The arrival of the Kansas colony in Walla Walla sparked a great deal of interest in a local newspaper. The editors of the paper were impressed that the immigrants were traveling to settle the regions surrounding Endicott and Plainville "where they will settle, having already secured places for location." By wagon trails and iron rails the colonists came to the region: "A part of the colony go by wagon from Portland, the others by rail." When they arrived at Texas Ferry, Tannatt's agents helped them across the river and complete their journey to their new home. Indeed

Tannatt was instrumental in aiding the Volga Germans, and it was reported that, "Every help possible will be given these people by General Tannatt and his subordinates."[9] The interaction between Tannatt and the Germans was close and extremely significant to the successful settlement of the Palouse Country by the immigrants. According to the editor of the Walla Walla *Statesman,* the immigrants first visited the office of the Oregon Improvement Company. When the editor journeyed to that office he reported:

Calling at the office of the Oregon Improvement Company on Monday to introduce gentlemen from the East we found quite a delegation to whom General Tannatt was explaining the Palouse Country and arranging for settlement. Some weeks since a portion of this Kansas Colony was met by the Oregon Improvement Company's teams at Texas Ferry and are now building on lands purchased of the Com. The portion of the Colony now here, with their own teams will be met by additional teams at Texas Ferry, to carry out household goods sent by train. Gen. Tannatt will meet them in Endicott, to complete contracts and outer houses built for their use. This organized method of handling immigrants is doing much for the Palouse Country, directly and indirectly for all of eastern Washington. The ample capital of the Oregon Improvement Company and their simple method of dealing promptly with newcomers, upon an easily understood plan, is most proper — Mr. Greene who is with those who left on Saturday says twenty-four families are on the way hither and those now at Endicott are much pleased with the country and their reception.[10]

Large tents were staked out for the newcomers in the bustling young community of Endicott which had grown rapidly since it had been platted by the Oregon Improvement Company early in 1882. The town was named for one of its directors, William Endicott, Jr. and an ambitious building campaign was launched through the resident Oregon Improvement Company agent, John Courtright.[11] Phillip Green was one of the first immigrants to arrive in the area and his first experiences there are indicative of other immigrants who settled the Palouse Country. One of Green's first activities was to fashion an earthen home in a hillside on his farm, similar to the *zemlyanki* dug by the first German colonists on the Volga, and Indians were blamed for stealing his horses shortly after their arrival.[12] Enduring a difficult

141

winter, he hauled lumber from Colfax the following spring and built a four room house.[13] To supplement his income, Green, like many others, went to work on the construction of the Palouse line of the Northern Pacific Railroad. Some of the men were accompanied by their families who lived in tents. The rails reached Colfax in 1883 and grading continued toward Pullman and Moscow.[14]

Tannatt further reported that the settlers were learning a great deal about their new home and how to tend the land. In a graphic description of the early farming, Tannatt stated the following.

Seeding in the Palouse Country as late as June 1 with certainty of crops. This season being measurably backward we can seed as late as June and continue plowing for fall sowing much later. The policy of buying but a limited number of teams has proven itself correct. Our teams have been fully employed up to plowing season in hauling lumber and fencing. The Co. have now erected Boarding house, Company Building, Smith Shop, tool shed and three cottages (in Endicott).

Grain for feed. Spring and fall sowing was brought in early fall at an extreme low figure is well cleaned and sacked. Seven acres are just in garden which will supply us with potatoes and in ample quality. Temporarily our lands are isolated. The advancement of line from Snake River to Willow Springs have left our lands in a position where immigration cannot reach them except when entering Washington Territory from the East with their own teams.[15]

Adding new impetus to regional development was the final completion of the Northern Pacific Railroad on September 8, 1883 when the gap was closed on the transcontinental line at Gold Greek, Montana. More Volga Germans came to the area, and in the fall of 1883, Mrs. Green's father, Henry Rothe, arrived with his daughter. Unfortunately for the family, Rothe died within two weeks. Other Volga Germans who came to the region were Henry Repp, his wife Mary, and Mary's sister, Anna Litzenberger, the families of John Helm, John and George Schreiber, Conrad Wilhelm, and John Peter Ochs. Within five years of the completion of the Northern Pacific line, other Volga German families who immigrated to Whitman County included those of Conrad and Peter Aschenbrenner, Henry Fisher, Christian Hagen,

Conrad Kammerzell, Christian and Henry Kleweno, George P. Litzenberger, Conrad Machleit, and Adam Weitz.[16] As one family settled in the Palouse Country, they wrote their friends and families still living in other parts of the world and encouraged them to migrate to the Pacific Northwest. In its widely distributed 1883 guidebook, the Northern Pacific was hailing the Palouse Country as

> One of the most fertile and extensive agricultural regions on the Pacific Coast. The Palouse country extends from the base of the Coeur d'Alene Mountains westward sixty miles, so is partly in Idaho, and it reaches northwardly from Snake River seventy-five to 100 miles. The railroad will push east to the mountains nearly 100 miles, with branches to Moscow, Idaho, and Farmington, W.T. West of the Palouse there is very little arable land, but east of that stream is a fertile country of the best description. *Endicott* is a new town that the road will develop. It is in the midst of a farming country not yet settled and cultivated. The chief town in this region is *Colfax,* which has hitherto been the centre of business. *Moscow* is the terminus of the southeast branch of the road. It has the mountains for its eastern background, and a rich surrounding country that will build up its prosperity.
>
> The same is true of *Farmington,* twenty-five miles to the northward, to which another branch will extend. The Palouse region consists of a rolling surface of country, with rich soil even on the highest hill tops. There is no timber on its prairies, but abundance of it along the streams and on the mountains.[17]

Villard's empire fell victim to increasing financial pressures, and in December, 1883 he was forced to relinquish control of the Oregon Railway and Navigation Company as well as the Northern Pacific, both of which reverted to separate private control. Under new management the Palouse branch of the Northern Pacific pushed on in April, 1885 from Colfax to Pullman, Washington and Moscow, Idaho. In the following year, the railroad reached the budding farm communities of Garfield, Tekoa, and Farmington — where General Tannatt moved in 1888, living on a large farmstead. Through his recommendation, many Volga Germans found temporary employment with the railroad or at his Farmington ranch.[18]

Their exposure to these other areas led many to homestead throughout Whitman County. Volga German settlement expanded to many of the towns serviced by the railroad including Farmington, Garfield, Steptoe and Colfax,

143

which later harbored its own "Russian Town" in the city's northeast section along First Street. In the summer of 1888 an immense railroad bridge was built at Riparia spanning the Snake River which allowed the Oregon Railway and Navigation Company to reach its Columbia and Palouse line at LaCrosse. Spokane was reached in 1889 from Tekoa, and the Palouse country was totally encircled that year when a feeder line from Winona to Farmington by way of Oakesdale and St. John was completed.[19] The Volga Germans were greatly influenced by the railroad. Many traveled to their new homes by rail, many were first employed by the railroad, many settled in towns serviced by the trains, and all of them depended on the railroad to transport their crops to markets.

One million acres of potential crop land were said to be within the revised 1883 boundary of Whitman County which conformed then to its present shape. The Volga German settlers from Kansas were anxious to establish a colony within Whitman County and they set out to find a suitable site. Shortly after Conrad Schierman arrived in the Palouse, he rode horseback north from Endicott to explore the surrounding countryside.[20] Waves of knee-high tawny bunchgrass blew in the breeze across the broad hills. After riding about five miles, he came to the crest of a massive basaltic bluff overlooking the Palouse River Valley. Finding it too steep to descend, he followed the river's course upstream until he came to a more gentle slope near its northernmost point in that area. Descending here and riding back a short distance to the expanse spied earlier, he found a beautiful tableland bordered on the west by the river and sheltered on the east by the steep rock bluffs. He returned to the railroad camp and shared the news of his discovery with the other families who proceeded to investigate the site together. They were taken by the beauty and fertility of the site, and therefore they traveled to the federal land office in Colfax to arrange for the purchase of the land. Their request was rather unorthodox since it was their intention to collectively purchase the quarter-section of land on the river. However it was divided equally, which reflected the *mir* model to which they had been accustomed in Russia.[21]

144

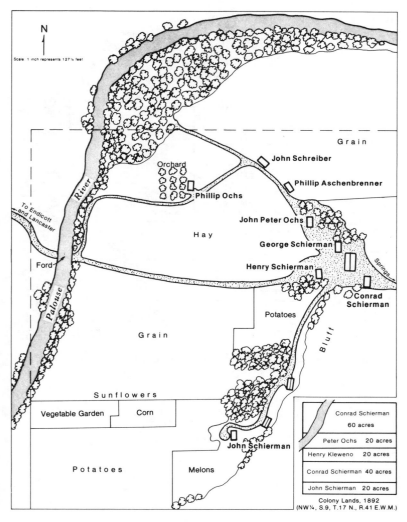

Palouse Colony, 1884

Map 7. The Volga German Palouse Colony, 1884.

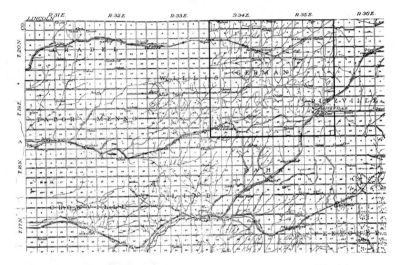

Map 8. The "German" townships of Adams County, Washington.

146

The colony consisted of the Peter and Henry Ochs families together with those of Conrad, Henry, George, and John Schierman. John Schierman became the group's treasurer and chief carpenter. Other Volga Germans joined these families in the small collective, including John Schreiber and Phillip Aschenbrenner.[22] Daily life in the commune was busy for both parents and children, as everyone assisted in the building of the first eight homes which were simple, but adequate, three-room structures.

It soon became apparent that with the abundance of prime farmland and mechanized methods of cultivation, an individual could acquire and manage larger estates in relative self-sufficiency. In later years, therefore, this fact led members of the Palouse Colony to move away from the colony and to purchase their own farms. Others, however, chose to pursue business ventures in neighboring towns that served the interests of the agrarian populace. The original Palouse Colony soon became a clearing house for newly arriving Volga Germans, serving as a temporary residence until they located nearby. One example of an immigrant who settled in the Palouse country was John Peter Ochs who had remained in Kansas but migrated to the Palouse Colony in 1883 only after his cousins had done so. He added greatly to the colorful history of the Palouse Colony. The sound of his melodic whistle filled the air of the colony as he worked in the fields. In the evenings his voice echoed throughout the valley in which the colony was nestled as he sang the familiar German hymns.[23]

It was a difficult task for adults and children alike to leave their homes on the Volga and migrate to a foreign land. Naturally they had some fears and anxieties about the far-off lands of America, but parents were convinced that their move to the United States would benefit the family significantly. To convince their children and perhaps themselves that the overseas move was in their best interest as well, mothers and fathers, grandmothers and grandfathers told the children fascinating tales of America — "the land where milk and honey flows." Shortly after their arrival in the area, the children would steal the wild honey from hollow trees along

147

the Palouse River and herd the cows home each evening, their udders bulging with milk after grazing in the thick green pastures. Then the parents reminded them, "Look - see, you have the milk flowing from the cows and the honey flowing from the trees, just like we said it would be like here when we were in Russia."[24] A large spring and brook provided all the water needed for the colony, and farming was confined at first to large gardens of potatoes, corn, and melons. The settlers soon found that wheat and barley grew particularly well on the chestnut brown soil as well as oats which were planted on the areas bordering the bluffs. The sowing of these crops was all done by hand broadcasting. They had come to be well acquainted with the cultivation of these grains in Russia and they learned a great deal from other farmers whom they met through their dealings with the Oregon Improvement Company. Much practical information was gained on their trips to Colfax or Walla Walla where they purchased food, hardware, and clothing.

The colony expanded as they planted an orchard of fruit trees and started a small herd of cattle. The pasture land was thick with wild grasses in the spring and summer and the herd prospered rapidly. A watchful eye was ever focused on the livestock as they grazed along the river since large packs of coyotes roamed the hills and cougars were a common sight on the rocky precipices. Phillip Schierman was made quite aware of their presence when one boldly attacked him while he was riding horseback one evening. Luckily, he escaped with only minor cuts and a clawed rifle stock to verify his ordeal.

One of the greatest threats to the cattle proved to be the huge flocks of sheep that grazed along the river. As was the case on several American frontiers, problems arose when these animals were grazed in the same area. Indeed, as many as five thousand sheep moved through the valley at a time and clipped the grass almost to the root. The livestock situation in the Palouse countryside was graphically illustrated in 1885 by the following newspaper account.[25]

General Tannatt as general agent of the Oregon Railway and Navigation Company has collected the following figures, not counting small farmers owning from 10 to 15 head of cattle: Taking Endicott as a center there are within a radius of twelve miles, 75,250 sheep, 3,562 head of cattle, 5,395 horses, 8,176 acres of land under cultivation and 1,510 acres in improved hay lands.

Many Indians of the Palouse bands often passed the settlement enroute to the ranches of Steve Cutler and the McCrosky brothers, several miles upstream, where they traded salmon for fruits and meat. Particularly fond of Mrs. Aschenbrenner's biscuits, they often stopped to barter but often succeeded only in frightening the women. In a minor incident in the 1880s, the J. H. Lairds, a pioneer family of 1872, was compelled to flee their home near the river and seek refuge in the colony when several Indians forced their way into their house. Laird returned with several members of the colony to his farm a short distance downstream to find the house abandoned but in complete disarray.[26]

The chief task of the Russian German settlers was always farming. The warm weather brought on by spring marked the time for them to begin plowing, and the first turning of the sod was extremely difficult because of the fibrous root system of the native vegetation. The men used as many as six horses to pull the single shear of the walking plow which constantly had to be cleared of the roots which collected on it. It took days to plow a few acres of ground, and following this operation, the seed was sowed by hand from horseback or on foot. Harrowing the field with a crude wooden implement completed the process until the summer harvest.

Improvements in farm equipment enabled farmers in the Pacific Northwest to increase productivity and manage larger acreages. Mechanical broadcasters and self-rake reapers were introduced to the region about 1884, both of which allowed the operator to cover a significantly larger area in the long work day.[27] Seeding by broadcast and harrowing was not an effective method in the drier areas of the inland Northwest since the seed often laid for weeks in the dry chernozem soil before seasonal rains induced germination. The appearance of the mechanical shoe drill by 1890 and the later disc drill marked important advancements in agricultural mechanization as the seed could then be deposited in uniform rows below the surface nearer to the moisture level.

149

The annual harvest was another project which involved the gathering of the grain stalks in the field where they were forked into wagons and taken to a centralized location. Prior to the use of the reaper, which cut and tied the grain into bundles, a cradle was used in cutting. As had been done in Russia, the families then gathered to flail the piles of grain, or it was placed on the ground and the work horses were led around a pole in a circle to trample the golden particles out of the heads. The farmers would then wait for a moderate wind and toss it into the air to blow away the chaff.[28]

Early varieties of wheat raised by the pioneers in the Inland Empire were two spring strains, Little Club and Pacific Bluestem, followed by the winter varieties, Red Russian and Turkey Red. A crop of forty-five bushels per acre was a typical yield, and often as much as twenty bushels per acre could be gleaned from a crop volunteer.[29] One of the major problems faced by these early farmers was working the steep slopes of the Palouse hills. This was extremely difficult with the primitive equipment but it was soon found that the grain grew just as well on the hilltops and that the hills had the advantage of having less risk of frost than the lowlands.

Settlers continued flocking to the Inland Empire by the thousands during these years, and regional population growth led to the new jurisdictional changes. In 1883, Whitman and Spokane counties were detatched from the Big Bend, forming the counties of Adams, Lincoln, Franklin, and Douglas. The town of Sprague was the principal shipping and receiving station for the area and the town maintained its importance until the Northern Pacific Railroad began construction on its trunk line into the fertile upper Big Bend near the end of the decade.

Members of the Nebraska colony, who had wintered in Walla Walla after their arrival in 1882, continued working in the area at various means of livelihood. Meanwhile, they investigated various options for collective settlement in the area. Some of the Volga Germans of the colony including Dewalds, Schoesslers, Schaefers, Heimbigners, and others, decided to remain in Walla Walla which was blossoming into a major trade center for the region. They recognized the potential of the community which grew to a population of 3,588 by 1888. A visitor to Walla Walla that year reported:

> The people were bright, intelligent and pleasant to meet, but not without the ambitious and pregressive natures of other places we had visited. The feeling of self satisfaction, possessing the thought that Walla Walla was the hub of the universe, was like the old feeling of the Bostonian for his beloved Boston.[30]

In the final stage of their quest for land, a large segment of the Nebraska colony was induced to settle near Ritzville, the community Phillip Ritz had developed. In the spring of 1883 the Nebraska colony of Volga Germans left Walla Walla in wagons and traveled on the Colville Road to Ritzville. The party included the families of Henry Amen, Sr., Hölfrich Bauer, Henry Kanzler, Sr., Conrad Kiehn, Henry Miller, Frederick Rosenoff, Jacob Thiel, Sr., and Conrad Wolsborn.[31] These immigrants were just a few of the many who were moving into the region. The April, 1882 issue of *The West Shore,* an early regional magazine, noted that the land around Ritzville "is rapidly being settled upon now, though the general opinion until last fall was that it was of little value for agriculture. Mr. Ritz and a few others have practically demonstrated that the idea was erroneous....The roads leading into the Big Bend are dotted with emigrant wagons."[32]

The Volga German families located on half sections about five miles northwest of Ritzville, but the men had to make a three-day journey to Colfax to file their claims. Most immigrants homesteaded while others purchased railroad land or filed timber culture claims on the treeless prairies. The loam was dark and rich in the area, but without lumber they had to live in sod houses or dugouts and use sagebrush and cow dung for fuel. Through efficient methods of tillage and fallowing, the industrious farmers achieved remarkable success. "Good houses, orchards, windbreaks, and windmills already made them a distinctive island in the semi-arid pioneer landscapes of Adams County."[33]

Of those remaining in Walla Walla, a small group led by John C. Oestreich moved in 1884 to the Horse Heaven country near Bickleton, Washington in Klickitat County. Again traveling by wagons, this party included the families of Jacob Bastrom, George Jacob Dewald, John F. Kembel, Henry F. Michel, and Conrad Schaefer. Most of the men filed on homesteads and many raised livestock. Wild horses ranged in large herds throughout the area, and the settlers often traded them with the neighboring Klickitat Indians. Some of the early Volga Germans settlers who raised livestock and began the first farming in the area were the Schoesslers, Heimbigners, and Ekhardts. Many of these people told their relatives of the Northwest and were joined by them as a result. Some who went to Klickitat County, including the John F. Kembels and Henry Oestreichs, relocated to Ritzville about 1890 as Volga German settlement there was rapidly expanding into the Marcellus district and southeast of Odessa.[34]

Communication between the settlers and their families in the Midwest and Russia facilitated immigration as many forwarded to relatives the necessary funds for travel which were then paid off in labor or cash following their settlement in the region. Furthermore, with the completion of the Northern Pacific transcontinental line in 1883, the company intensified its advertising campaign to attract immigrants to the area. The guide distributed by the Northern Pacific Railroad, Oregon Railway and Navigation Company, and Oregon and California Railroad contained the following description of a portion of the lower Pend Oreille division along which many Germans from Russia settled:

Sprague — (148 miles from Heron; population, 1,100.) — This is a place of importance, being the headquarters of the Pend d'Oreille Division of the railroad. Here the railroad company has a large building for its offices, workshops and a roundhouse, and employs several hundreds of workmen in car building, repairing, etc. Sprague is also within easy reach of good agricultural country in all directions, and does a flourishing trade. The place almost rivals Jonah's gourd, that came up in a night. It was a vacant space in the autumn of 1881, but now it is a favorite resort of immigrants, being situated centrally to the fertile regions north of the Snake River and along the railroad....

Ritzville — (117 miles from Heron.) — This is the starting point of what is likely to be a town of importance in the course of

Fig. 40. Mr. and Mrs. Caspar Külthau, early Portland residents from Norka.

Fig. 41. Volga German colony on the Palouse River, c. 1895.

Fig. 42. Endicott, Washington, c. 1910. (Luke Benner)

Bird's eye view of Endicott.
— 14. Photo by Hutchison.

Fig. 43. Ritzville, Washington, 1908.

Fig. 44. Odessa, Washington, 1900.

Fig. 45. Boenig & Labes Warehouse, Lind, Washington, c. 1902.

158

Fig. 46. Heimbigner family hauling grain near Odessa, c. 1920. (Bernice Elledge)

Fig. 47. Conrad Kissler and daughter Catherine plowing near Odessa, c. 1910. (Bernice Elledge)

Fig. 48. St. John, Washington, 1904. (Washington State University Libraries)

Fig. 49. Colfax, Washington, 1905.

Wacker & Schafer's Combined-Harvester,
Odessa, Wash. Aug. 7, 1909.

Fig. 50. Wacker and Schafer's combined-harvester, Odessa, Washington, 1907. (Collection of Henry J. Amen)

163

SACK PILE THRESHED BY MOORE BROS. 1911 CROP. 933 SACKS. 2200 BU. PHOTO BY HUTCHISON.

Fig. 51. Moore Bros. sack pile near Endicott, 1911. (Washington State University Libraries)

Fig. 52. Poffenroth threshing crew near De Winton, Alberta, 1939.

Fig. 53. Tacoma, Washington, c. 1890. (Washington State University Libraries)

Fig. 54. Quincy, Washington, 1911.

Fig. 55. Wenatchee Valley, Washington, c. 1920.

Fig. 56. The J. Conrad Frank family, pioneer Walla Walla residents from Kautz, Russia. (Elaine Davison)

time. As yet immigration goes further north, and shuns the dry hills and plains below Sprague. The future will show that much of this soil is fertile, and well worth cultivation.[35]

Recurrent waves of immigrants responded to newly opened regions, and by 1888 town of Ritzville had sufficiently developed for its residents to seek incorporation. In the same year a post office and store were opened in Lind. In the late 1880s, Walla Walla experienced the continued influx of immigrants from Walter, Walter Khutor, Frank, and Hussenbach. In time many of them congregated in that section of Walla Walla which became appropriately known as *"die russische Ecke,"* (the Russian Corner) or "Little St. Petersburg," extending between Chase and Second Streets from Willard to Chestnut. Another enclave in the city was near the German Congregational Church by Ninth and Birch streets.[36]

It will be recalled that Phillip Green's father, George Henry, remained in Portland with his wife and others in 1883 while the rest of the colony journeyed to Endicott. Between 1888 and 1890 Portland witnessed a considerable movement of Volga Germans from the Volga colonies of Balzer and Frank to Portland. This was followed by an even larger influx of those from Norka between 1890 and 1895.[37] Many joined the earlier arrivals living in Albina which was incorporated into Portland in 1891.

The ward around Northeast 7th Avenue and along Union Avenue from Freemont to Shaver Streets in Portland became a "Little Russia." This area of Portland was filled by the enterprising Volga Germans who began such business establishments as Repp Brothers' Meat and Groceries, Hildermann's Groceries, Hergerts' Meat Market, Geist Shoe and Department Store, Trupp Shoe Repair, and Weimer's Hardware and Furniture. Among the earliest Volga German immigrants to the district was Conrad Schwartz, George and John Betz, Adam, Conrad and Constantine Brill, Frank and Henry Meier, Adam and David Schwind, the Repps, Popps and Millers.[38] As forests were cleared around the city, some of these people moved south to Canby. In 1892 Catholic Volga Germans from Semenowka and Köhler began settling in Portland while others located in Toppenish, Washington.[39]

It was not until 1888 that the Northern Pacific Railroad began efforts for the construction of its upper Big Bend branch which was dubbed the "Washington Central." When completed, the line ran westward from Cheney through Davenport, Wilbur, Almira, Hartline, and on to Coulee City. This line facilitated immigration into the area which was known to be rich and desirable farmland. The average annual rainfall was greater in this higher country and the soil was correspondingly richer. It is understandable, then, that the entire area from Davenport to the Grand Coulee had been settled prior to the construction of the Washington Central branch.[40] The completion of James J. Hill's Great Northern transcontinental railroad into the Big Bend country in 1892 virtually bisected the Northern Pacific's service lines in the area, facilitating new settlement along the Great Northern's Crab Creek route at such newly platted sites as Harrington, Mohler, Odessa, Krupp (Marlin), and Wilson Creek.[41] Odessa's name reflected the great number of Russian Germans who were locating in that vicinity while other names indicative of Russian immigrant presence in the area included Batum, Schrag, Tiflis, and Moscow (Bluestem).[42] In the drier areas of the western Big Bend, the climate combined with the imperiled national economy of the 1890s to inhibit settlement there until the turn of the century. In Grant County, Ephrata was platted in 1901 as was Quincy in the following year.

The Weber family pioneered Volga German settlement near Quincy in 1902. Adam Weber had emigrated from Walter Khutor, Russia to Walla Walla 1889 where he engaged in farm labor until he obtained land near Ritzville. He was joined there by his brother, Jacob, in 1901 and in the following year by their father, John Adam, and other brothers, Christian and Henry. All but Adam, (he joined them later) filed on quarters in the same section of land near Quincy in the spring of 1902 and began irrigating from a single well put in the middle of their property. It was difficult to begin farming the dry, sandy loam and Conrad later remarked that he thought of leaving the area more than once "but we were too poor to get away, though we had plenty to eat and feed for our stock, as well as a roof over our heads."[44]

Jacob Weber relocated in 1909 to the famous orcharding district of the Wenatchee Valley near Dryden, where Bessarabian Germans had settled soon afterwards. Other Russian Germans later settled at Peshastin, Cashmere, and Wenatchee. The number of first generation Russian Germans in Grant County swelled at approximately 377 in 1920 while Chelan County registered 68.[45] In 1916, Conrad Lautenschlager filed a homestead claim on land which had just been opened on the Colville Indian Reservation near the mouth of the Okanogan River. Lautenschlager was a native of Jagodnaja Poljana, Russia who had immigrated with his family in 1900 to Wisconsin and eventually to Endicott, Washington. He "broke out" the reservation land for wheat and pasture in 1916 while the family remained in Endicott until the following spring when they joined him and established a Volga German presence in that scenic region of north central Washington near Brewster.[46]

In the late 1890s demand grew in the world market for soft winter wheat. This brought a new prosperity to the Inland Northwest since the region was well adapted to the growing of this crop and rapidly being settled. These factors, combined with the negative effects of Russia on the Russian Germans arising out of the previously detailed Ukase of 1892 and recurrent crop failures prompted more to leave their homeland. During this decade an interesting corollary to great northwest Volga German settlement occurred. The movement to Alberta, Canada began with the arrival in the Palouse Colony in the spring of 1891 of the Peter Poffenroths, the Henry B. and Adam Scheuermans, and Adam Schmick. This group had all departed their native colony of Jagodnaja Poljana in the spring of 1888 and endured together with other "Yagaders" the Atlantic voyage in May on the *S.S. Hungaria* from Hamburg to New York.[47]

After spending three years in the vicinity of Florence and Newton, Kansas some of them decided to join friends in Washington. Arriving in Endicott in March, 1891 the Poffenroths, Scheuermans, and Adam Schmick boarded in a three-room dwelling in the Palouse Colony until they found farms of their own.[48] Emigrants arriving from Jagodnaja Poljana the following year included several other Poffenroths, all brothers who settled at Moscow, Idaho: Christian, Henry, George, and Peter.[49] The summer of 1892 was particularly hot and dry, severely damaging the crops and Adam Scheuerman, who was renting a farm, resolved to personally investigate settlement possibilities in Canada where it was rumored good land was still open for sale at reasonable terms.

Although the Canadian Pacific Railroad had been completed in 1886, Scheuerman found it cheaper to join four other men, not Volga Germans, in a long trek north led by a prospector enroute to the Kootenai goldfields. Scheuerman's son, John, also accompanied the party as they loaded his father's breaking plow into a wagon and set off with seven horses to points northward in what was intended to be a three-week journey. Had they foreseen the struggles ahead, an alternate route probably would have been chosen. The road they took led them north of Spokane into the Rocky Mountains but soon deteriorated into a rocky trail impassable for the wagon. Not to be defeated, they constructed a large raft to hold two of the men and the wagon while the Scheuermans continued on horseback over the rugged terrain. John nearly drowned several times while testing the depths of the swollen rivers with a rope tied to his horse and anchored to shore.

After weeks of arduous travel and near drownings, they finally emerged from the mountain wilderness at Banff, both horses and men facing starvation. They managed to meet the two men with the wagon and continued north to Wetaskiwin, Alberta arriving six weeks after leaving Endicott. Scheuerman filed for a homestead on unsurveyed land thirty miles southeast of the town near the present site of Bashaw.[50] He went to work on the construction of the railroad between Edmonton and Calgary at 50ᶜ a day and, not wanting the rest of his family to endure the same trip, procured free passes for them on the railroad. They lived in a cave-like enclosure on the farm the first winter subsisting largely on wild rabbits for meat.[51]

The Henry Scheuermans also arrived in Canada in 1892,

homesteading a quarter section southwest of Red Deer Lake next to Adam's property. More adequate buildings were constructed the next year and a large influx of foreign immigration to the area began in 1894, much from the province of Volhynia in Russia though later settlers were also from the Volga.[52] The newcomers organized a congregation, St. Peter's Church, in 1897 under the auspices of the newly formed German Evangelical Lutheran Synod of Manitoba and a beautiful country church was erected in 1903.

Volga German immigration to Calgary was also hastened in 1894 as the four Poffenroth brothers — Christian, Henry, George, and Peter — together with John Geier and others moved there after emigrating from Jagodnaja Poljana to Endicott. Land was more readily available in Alberta where, under Canada's 1872 land law, individuals could secure title to 160 acres for a mere $10 registration fee and three years' residence. This factor, together with the availability of Canadian Pacific Railroad land induced many to settle in the Pine Creek district near De Winton. Plantings were confined to the spring due to the harsh winters and many found employment in the city. In 1902 the Volga Germans organized Emmanuel Lutheran Church in the Riverside area of Calgary which became known as "Little Yagada" (after the mother colony Jagodnaja Poljana) and by 1913 it was estimated that nearly one thousand Germans were living in Calgary, most in the Riverside district.[53] Many came direct from Russia through such Canadian ports of entry in the East as Halifax, Nova Scotia.

About the turn of the century Volga Germans from Kolb began settling in Tacoma where they found employment in sawmills and factories. Among the first to go there was George Miller who had immigrated earlier to Hastings, Nebraska, where he heard of the opportunities for work in the Pacific Northwest. He journeyed west about 1899 to Tacoma and was soon joined by other Volga Germans from Kolb, many of whom had worked in the Ritzville area until the harvest season was over. Other early emigrants to Tacoma included Peter and John Jacob Koch, Peter Miller, and a Yukert family.

Later Volga German arrivals there were families named Achziger, Adler, Bauer, Meininger, Muench, Rehn, Reiber, Ruth, Thaut, Thorn, and Wilhelm. Although they were predominantly from Kolb, others also came from Frank, Hussenbach, Walter, and Dönhoff.[54] This group established a beautiful neighborhood of white houses dotted with their churches, known as "Little Russia," between South 19th and 23rd Streets along Ainsworth, Cushman, and Sheridan Avenues.[55] After the turn of the century a considerable Volga German nucleus formed in Bellingham with most of the men employed in lumber mills. George Schmidt, a native of Frank, was among the first to arrive there from Russia, coming in 1885. However, he later relocated to Walla Walla.

In Eastern Washington the population in the Big Bend country continued to rise during the first decade of the new century; the totals are taken from the 1910 census: Ritzville, 1,859; Lind, 831; Odessa, 885; Sprague, 1,100; Harrington, 661; Davenport, 1,229; Wilbur, 757; Ephrata, 323; Quincy, 264 and Wilson Creek, 405. The influx of Black Sea Germans between 1900 and 1905 was particularly heavy to the districts of Odessa, Ritzville, Krupp, Ruff, Wheeler, Warden, Ralston, Packard, and Lind,[56] and Russian German settlement in the next decade continued to Cashmere, Peshastin, and Dryden in the Wenatchee Valley.[57]

The Palouse country witnessed a similar growth during the same period involving many Volga Germans, although a number of Black Sea Germans who had immigrated earlier to Parkston, South Dakota relocated about 1905 in the vicinity between Colfax and LaCrosse near Dusty. In 1910 Colfax, the county seat, contained 2,783 inhabitants, Endicott had 474, and Volga Germans continued to settle between there and St. John to the north which had 421 residents in 1910.[58]

Walla Walla grew to nearly 20,000 inhabitants by 1910 as Volga German immigration to that city continued through the first two decades of the new century and by 1920 approximately 715 first generation Russian Germans lived in the country.[59] Most were still coming from Walter, Walter Khutor, and Hussenbach although emigration to Walla Walla from Kautz had begun around the turn of the century.

175

State	Black Sea Germans		Volga Germans		Mennonites	First Generation Total	1st & 2nd Generation Total
	Evangelical	Catholic	Evangelical	Catholic			
Washington	4,500	1,500	5,000	375	500	4,933	11,875
Oregon	281	1,000	3,750	1,000	1,000	3,281	7,031
Idaho	1,224	——	800	——	500	1,025	2,524
Total	6,005	2,500	9,550	1,375		9,239	21,430

TABLE II: RUSSIAN GERMAN GROUPS IN THE PACIFIC NORTHWEST, 1920 (Sallet, P. 112)

Some of the families from Kautz later joined relatives in Laurel, Montana where many had found employment following the construction of a large beet sugar refinery at nearby Billings in 1906.[60] Volga German immigration to these and other points in the Pacific Northwest continued unabated until 1914 when war broke out in Europe and decreased to an insignificant number after the 1917 Bolshevik Revolution. Russia became embroiled in a Civil War and the victorious Bolshevik later restricted travel over the borders.

In the spring of 1917, the U & I sugar company recruited Russian German laborers from the Ritzville and Odessa areas to work in the beet fields of the Yakima Valley near Toppenish, Wapato, and Union Gap. A number of Volga German families were grateful for the opportunity to find work there including those of William Eichler, George and Henry Wuertenberger, George Wortt, and George Kissler. Most of these families originally came from the villages of Frank and Neu Dönhoff.[61] By 1920 there were about 500 first generation Russian Germans living in Yakima County.

Russian Germans living in the three Pacific Northwest states by 1920 numbered approximately 21,480, contributing to an impressive national total of over 303,000. About one-third of this number (118,493) had come from the Volga[62] and in several Washington counties (see Table III) Volga Germans amounted to over 30% of the total foreign born element.[63] Clearly, the Volga Germans had made a major impact in the region during the dynamic era of pioneer settlement, playing an integral role in the development of business and agriculture in the Pacific Northwest.

6

PIONEERING MISSION WORK

Glaube der Väter, heil'ge Glut
Zum Liebesdienst im Kampfe hier
Dich fünden wir dem Freund und Feind
Durch sanftes Wort un Tugendzier.
Faith of our fathers, we will love
Both friend and foe in all our
strife:
And preach thee, too, as love
knows how,
By kindly words and virtuous
life.
— "Glaube der Väter," v. 3
Traditional

The Volga Germans continued to be devout people in America. As their numbers grew in the Midwest, they perpetuated their faith through associations with several denominations, and as immigration streamed to the Pacific Northwest during the 1880s, they established churches there as well. Approximately 85% of the Volga Germans who settled in Oregon, Washington, and Idaho were Protestant and the remainder were Catholic.[1] Of the Protestants, the majority continued to be Lutheran although the German Congregational Church also developed into an important denomination among the Volga Germans. Other Russian Germans joined the Methodist, Episcopal, Reformed, and Seventh-Day Adventist Churches. It was German Congregationalism, however, that gained the earliest religious prominence among Volga Germans in the Pacific Northwest, as its missionaries were most readily available to the German immigrant population. Furthermore, its doctrinal position was well adapted to alleviate disputes which the German pietists had known in Russia.[2]

The German Department of the Congregational

Churches had its inception in 1846 among German immigrants who had settled on the Iowa frontier. It was primarily occupied with missionary efforts to the scattered areas of settlement in the Midwest, but with the surge of immigration in the 1850s and 1860s, it soon became a leading force among German Protestants in America. The German Congregational Church held to traditional evangelical church doctrine while encouraging the free use of the German language in religious work. Of equal importance to the Volga German pietists, it held to the principle of the autonomous local church.[3] Elements of their religious fervor had long been thwarted by the Lutheran consistory in Russia, and it was thought by many that association with the Congregationalists would provide the opportunity for a fuller realization of the Christian faith.

It was Emmanuel Jose, a German Pietist from the Odessa District in Russia, who made the initial contact between the German Russian Pietists and the Congregationalists in America. Immigrating to America in 1874, he had been raised in the atmosphere of the brotherhood in Russia and continued to espouse its theology through his preaching in Nebraska and the Dakota Territory. He worked there with others supported by the American Home Missionary Society. Through the efforts of Jose and his associates a number of churches were organized among German immigrants in the Midwest; congregations composed entirely of Volga Germans were formed in 1880 in Sutton and Culbertson, Nebraska. In a report to the American Home Missionary Society in 1881, Rev. H. Hetzler described Jose's mission to the Volga Germans in Culbertson:

> I found quite a settlement of Russian-Germans....Most of these are homesteaders, on the vast prairies now Culbertson... Isolated, these people live in their sod-houses, scattered all over the prairie. Here they pray and sing praises to the Lord. Brother Jose, who resided in Sutton, served these people about once in three months. They are as sheep, having no fold and no shepherd. Not a church of any kind did I see in that whole region of country.[4]

As more churches were organized and received into the Congregational fellowship, the needs for more effective organization and qualified pastors became apparent. Crete Seminary in Nebraska was opened in 1878, followed four years later by the formation of the German Department of the Chicago Theological Seminary. In 1883 a General Conference was organized known as *Die Allgemeine Evangelische Kirchenversammlung der Deutschen Kongregationalisten,* altered to the General Conference of the German Congregational Churches in 1888.[5]

With the arrival of the Volga German Nebraska colony in Washington in 1882, German Congregationalism was carried to the Far West as well. The Volga Germans who settled near Ritzville in 1883 had encountered a pastor, Reverend F. Frucht. He ministered to their spiritual needs while they wintered in Walla Walla and gathered them into a church in 1882 which is considered the first German Congregational Church in the Pacific Northwest. It was permanently established near Ritzville. This church, however, existed as an independent organization until 1888 when it was officially received into the Congregational Church, adopting the name *Erste Deutsche Kongregational Kirche.*[6]

Through Pastor Frucht's missionary efforts several other congregations were organized in the area among Volga Germans. In 1883 a church was formed in Walla Walla, apparently by those Volga Germans who remained in the city, and in the same year Frucht organized a church in Endicott.[7] Volga German settlement at this latter location had begun in 1882 by members of the Kansas colony who were ministered to for a time by an English Congregationalist, Reverend Thomas W. Walters, resident pastor of Plymouth Church in Colfax.[8] By 1887 the membership of the German Congregational Church in Ritzville had grown to forty-three and in Endicott to twenty-two. However, in the same year Rev. Frucht withdrew from the district without a replacement proficient in German. The lamentable situation was evident in the Association's 1887 *Minutes:* "Pastor Frucht, who has served them (the Volga Germans) for some time, now leaves them, and they know not where to look for another pastor to lead them in their church work."[9] For them it was an act of providence when a Volga German pietist entered the field of Northwest Congregationalism the following spring.

A dynamic evangelist who had recently come from Russia, Johannes Koch arrived in Ritzville and accepted a pastoral call extended to him by the Volga Germans gathered there. He soon became acquainted with two prominent leaders of the Congregational Association of Washington Territory, Reverend Thomas W. Walters of Colfax and Reverend George H. Atkinson, who served as General Missionary and Superintendent of Home Missions. Since the English Congregationalists were not proficient in German but realized that large numbers of Russian Germans were settling in the region, they met with Koch in 1888 at Endicott and ordained him into the ministry of their church.[10]

This meeting marked the inception of German Congregationalism on the West Coast as Koch's churches in both Ritzville and Endicott were accepted into that fellowship at the time. As "Missionary of Pacific Coast," Koch became the leading force behind German Congregationalism in the American West and through his efforts hundreds of Germans from Russia became members of the Congregational Church. He served as pastor to churches in Ritzville (1888-91, 1893-95), Endicott (1888-93), Portland (1895-99), Ralston (1899-1904), and Sanger, California (1909-1912).[11]

Reflective of the revivalistic spirit engendered by Koch and others is this description written by Koch on February 6, 1893 of a series of meetings being held in Portland:

> We have not had a single evening without a meeting since Christmas. Last week our Brethren felt that the evenings would no longer suffice. We therefore had meetings hither and thither, beginning at nine o'clock every morning and closing at nine o'clock at night. People who were considered to be beyond the reach of grace have been carried along by the power of revival. Old perverse sinners, drunkards and hardened men; down to the age of fifteen, have been reached and humbly sought forgiving grace. Last Sunday we had reception of members. The church was packed full. Forty-eight converts gathered about the altar. All freely confessed Christ as their only Savior, after a very searching address. Then they were strongly exhorted to steadfastness in the Christian life and the Apostolic Confession of Faith was read to

them, to which they all responded with a loud 'yes'. Then while the church sang the hymm:

'To each other we give covenant
The faithful, fraternal hand'

I gave to each the right hand of fellowship. Then all went down on their knees, sometimes a half hour at a time. Every man wanted to thank the Lord that he had sought him and found him and given him his hand of fellowship...Thus the work goes on. God be praised![12]

In 1897 several Swiss and German congregations in the Northwest united with the Congregational Church, and this addition prompted the formation that year of the Pacific Conference. Embracing both Oregon and Washington, the first conference met on March 5 in Portland at the Ebenezer Church with fourteen delegates representing seven churches.

The following thirteen churches were received with their pastors into the newly formed conference: Alkali Flats (near LaCrosse, Washington), Ballard, Beaver Creek, Beaverton, Endicott, New Era (Oregon), Portland, Ritzville First, Ritzville Emmanuel, Ritzville Zion, Seattle, Stafford, and Walla Walla. Later in 1897 Rev. Gottfried Graedel organized a congregation northwest of Ritzville at Packard. In 1899 churches were organized in Quincy (Salem) and Ralston. Rev. J.C. Schwabenland pioneered missionary work in the Odessa area to which large scale German immigration from Russia began about 1900. In that year he organized the congregations of Odessa Pilgrim and Batum Hoffnungsberg. With the aid of Rev. Graedel, new churches were formed in 1902 including Marlin Zion and Odessa Friedensfeld. These two men ministered in this extensive field for many years and churches later established in the area included Odessa Emmaus (1904), Odessa Zoar (1904), Odessa Tabor (1907), and Odessa St. Matthews (1916).[13]

German Congregational membership continued to rise after the turn of the century and by 1910 it reached 1,249 in Oregon and Washington. In 1915 California was detached from the Pacific Conference to form its own division and by 1937 the Pacific Conference had grown to twenty-seven congregations with a total membership of 1,631.[14]

182

As was the case elsewhere in the nation though, most Volga Germans who settled in the Pacific Northwest remained Lutheran and became associated with several leading synods. Two of the largest German Lutheran bodies in the United States during the nineteenth century were the Joint Synod of Ohio and Other States and the German Evangelical Synod of Missouri, Ohio and Other States.[15] The Joint Synod, formed in 1818, was the second oldest Lutheran synod in America and was composed of both English and German speaking members.[16] (It later merged with the Buffalo and Iowa Synods to form the American Lutheran Church in August, 1930). The German Evangelical Synod of Missouri, Ohio and Other States (changed to Lutheran Church-Missouri Synod in 1947) was organized in 1847 and was also instrumental in forming the transition to American Lutheranism of many Russian German Lutherans. The efforts of both synods were directed primarily in the Midwest and East while their interest in expansion to the Pacific Northwest waned until the influx of Germans there in the late nineteenth century attracted their attention.

Both synods entered the field of Northwest missionary activity at the same time, and through the years their work was often typified by intense rivalry. Peculiar circumstances linked both groups with the inception of organized Lutheranism in the Northwest. Associated with the Joint Synod, Reverend Anders Fridrichsen arrived in Portland in 1871 and immediately began to gather Scandinavian Lutherans into a fellowship which resulted in the formation of the first Lutheran Church there that same year. Fridrichsen was of Norwegian background, but he did not limit this missionary work to Scandinavians. Indeed, he actively sought Germans and others as well. His repeated appeals to the synods in the East for more pastors had little effect. Finally, in 1876 Reverend August Kentner responded by resigning his Minnesota Synod pastorate and traveling to Oregon. He organized St. Paul's Lutheran Church in Sherwood under the auspices of the Missouri Synod. In 1878 this synod boasted the establishment of its first church in the Pacific Northwest.[17]

Reverend Edward Doering, who served a Missouri Synod congregation in the Chicago area, accepted a call to Oregon issued at the Western District Convention of 1880. He arrived in Portland in September, 1881 where he became increasingly interested in ministering to the Germans of the Portland area. Through his labors, Zion Lutheran Church was founded in the city of Portland. Doering soon became the prime mover in Northwest missionary work for the synod, traveling extensively throughout the region and serving at a multitude of scattered points of German settlement. In describing his character, one of Doering's fellow pioneer pastors remarked that he

> ...was a very modest, unassuming man, of simple habits. He was not graced with great oratorical gifts, but rather somewhat hampered in his enunciation by brogue, nevertheless by preaching the Gospel in its simple beauty, to the best of his ability, his efforts crowned with success. As he was of sound bodily health, and an indefatigable worker, he could quite regularly cover his large field.[18]

The Missouri Synod's position was further bolstered in 1882 when Fridrichsen's Portland Church was transferred to Missouri control in accordance with Fridrichsen's will. This situation arose out of the fact that the church building site was apparently owned by the pastor himself who, believing that the Joint Synod would not consider work in this distant field at that time, decided to will the church to the Missouri Synod which had already placed men in Oregon. This was accomplished shortly after his death in 1882 despite the opposition of some members in the congregation.[19]

The entrance of the Ohio Synod into Northwest religious affairs began in 1881 because of a doctrinal dispute with the Missouri Synod over its adoption of Dr. Walther's interpretation of predestination. This event caused a division among many clergy in the synod, resulting in the withdrawal of Dr. H.A. Allwardt, D.H. Ernst, C.H. Rohe, J.H. Doermann, and other prominent church officials. These men then became affiliated with the Joint Synod, which in 1882 established the Northwestern District with limits defined as "everything west of Chicago!" Allwardt was elected president; Ernst, vice-president; Doermann, secretary, and

J.L. Gruber, treasurer. Through the influence of these men, Luther Seminary was founded in Afton, Minnesota in 1885 (later moving to St. Paul and then merging with Wartburg Seminary at Dubuque, Iowa.). Under the tutelage of Professors H. Ernst and W. Schmidt at Luther Seminary, a number of pioneer Lutheran missionary pastors were supplied to the Pacific Northwest while others came from Capital University in Columbus, Ohio.[20]

By 1887 a synod publication indicated that the "boundless" Northwest District of the Joint Synod had taken on some definition, although this scarcely restricted its immensity. Appearing under "Miscellaneous", an article that year in the *Lutheran Standard* specified the Northwest District as "reaching from Duluth, Minn., to New Orleans, La., and from Michigan City, Ind., to New Tacoma, Washington Territory."[21] The outpost in Tacoma was the home of Frederick N. Wolf, a man later known to many as the "father of the German and English Lutheran Churches of Washington."[22] Pastor Wolf was called to this fertile mission field through Capital University by Empire German Lutheran families who emigrated from Ohio to Tacoma in the early 1880s. He accepted the call to this area of the Far West, void of any Lutheran clergy, and organized the first Lutheran church there, the Evangelical Trinity Congregation on March 22, 1884. A building was soon erected and dedicated on July 18, 1885.[23] (The second Joint Synod congregation in Tacoma was not organized until 1900 when Peace Lutheran Church was established among Volga Germans from Kolb, Russia under Pastor George Koehler.)[24] Inasmuch as Pastor Wolf was totally occupied with missionary activity in the Puget Sound area until his semi-retirement six years after his arrival, many enlarged their vision to the Inland Northwest where, as one pioneer Lutheran observer noted, three new towns were being platted every day![25]

At the Northwest District's sixth annual meeting in the spring of 1887 at Michigan City, Indiana, a traveling missionary recommended to the General Mission Board to be sent to Spokane Falls in Washington Territory. An interested

185

supporter immediately pledged a year's salary of three hundred dollars for such a man.[26] The missionary, Pastor Karl Anton Horn, responded to what was considered a Macedonian call issued through Mr. Henry Knostman who resided several miles north of Spokane Falls. This community in Eastern Washington was growing rapidly, and Knostman with other Lutherans had considered forming a church. However, they felt that the need for a pastor was essential. A petition was therefore forwarded to the Ohio Synod and Pastor Horn embarked on his journey in May of 1887.[27] Thus, he opened another field to Lutheranism in the Pacific Northwest.

Pastor Horn was originally from Saxony, Germany, born in 1855 in the village of Oberbobritzsdez near Freiberg. After attending the missionary seminary in Breklum, Schleswig-Holstein he accepted the call to the United States where he assisted Reverend Henry Rieke in his Wisconsin mission field.[28] Pastor Rieke, also a native of Germany, had arrived in America in 1884. He had been born in Döhren, Hannover and immigrated following the completion of his formal education at the missionary seminary in Hermannsburg. Rieke was accepted into the Joint Synod and established Cicero, Wisconsin as the center of his missionary endeavors. He was joined there by Pastor Horn who was ordained in the synod in 1887. These two men later played leading roles in pioneer missionary work among the German-speaking populace of the Northwest.[29]

Upon arriving at Spokane Falls in May, 1887 Pastor Horn immediately set out to minister to the needs of German immigrants throughout the region. In the manner of a traditional circuit rider, he preached at numerous towns including Spokane, Fairfield, Genesee, Colfax, Endicott, Walla Walla, Ritzville, and in the Marcellus district of Adams County. Pastor Rieke joined his former associate in the fall of 1887. For two years they ministered together as the only Joint Synod missionaries in the Inland Northwest, performing baptisms at the Palouse River Colony of Volga Germans near Endicott, administering the Sacraments to others who had homesteaded near Ritzville and organizing new groups in

186

Farmington and elsewhere. Reflective of the work undertaken by these and other early Lutheran missionaries is the following synopsis of "Fifteen Days in the Mission Field" of Eastern Washington beginning with Palm Sunday:

> In fifteen days we preached thirteen times, gave catechetical instuctions three times, one evening, one-half day, one full day; delivered four addresses; examined and confirmed a class of twelve catechumens; administered the Lord's Supper twice; baptized two children; visited sick four times; made two other calls; and to do this we had to travel 185 miles by team, 100 miles by train, and six to eight miles on foot.[30]

Later a member of the Idaho legislature, Reverend George Finke was also active in the early work of the Joint Synod in the Northwest. He described the joint ministry of the pathfinders Horn and Rieke in the following terms:

> A burning love for the savior filled their hearts, as well as the desire to bring lost souls to the Savior's feet. Pastor Horn, the Saxon, acted up to the royal command and would not pass a person on the road, or a house where people lived, without offering them salvation with Christ or damnation for their sins without Christ. His horse knew his master so well that he would not pass a gate without entering it. There is no doubt that many a person will confess on that day: 'I have found my Savior through the instrumentality of Horn.'

> Pastor Rieke, with his North-German organization talent was more for organizing congregations where the Gospel would find a home and souls could be drawn to the light of Christ. When he heard of any settlement of Lutherans, he went there with his message. No distance was too great, no road too bad (and we had bad roads here in the Northwest), no weather too stormy or cold or rainy, no snow too deep. Pastor Rieke did his duty, as our Lord expects us to do.[31]

The year 1887 marked the extension of mission work by the Missouri Synod into Eastern Oregon and Washington. Their pastors on the Pacific coast realized the need to form their own syndical district since the vast Western District was headquartered in St. Louis. Accordingly, a new district was organized at the Delegate Synod of 1887 held in Fort Wayne, Indiana and this Pacific District was further subdivided into Southern and Northern Conferences, the latter comprising Oregon and Washington. Frederick Selle, a candidate with the Synod, was called into service as their first resident mis-

187

sionary east of the Cascades in the Northern Conference, establishing his residence in Pendleton, Oregon.[32] Selle ministered to groups throughout the region, visiting Volga Germans in Eastern Washington until his work was interrupted by health problems. His health worsened and he died in 1888 while enroute for the East seeking treatment.[33] Pastor J.H. Theiss reported to the Synod Mission Board following a trip to the Inland Northwest in 1888 about the need for a replacement to continue the work. Later in the year, Candidate J. Ehlen was dispatched there although reasons of health also compelled him to suspend missionary activities within two years.[34] In the spring of 1890 Ehlen traveled to the coast enroute to California for recuperation but encountered a number of Lutherans in Tacoma who were without a pastor. They prevailed upon him to preach several sermons and through him Zion Lutheran Church was founded there in June 1890.[35] Rev. H. Haserodt became their first resident pastor later in the year as Ehlen continued on his trip to California where he died in Fresno shortly after his arrival. Again the Missouri Synod's work in Eastern Washington was interrupted at a time when additional men from the Joint Synod were entering service in the region.

With more and more of their time spent ministering to the widely dispersed groups in the area, Pastors Horn and Rieke of the Joint Synod welcomed the arrival to Spokane in August, 1889 of Reverend Paul F. Hein.[36] Pastor Rieke had resided in Spokane since 1888 but then moved to Genesee, Idaho. Pastor Horn had journeyed to The Dalles, Oregon and thus divided the vast field of Eastern Washington between himself and Rieke.[37] Reverend Hein also conducted missionary trips in the area while establishing his base in Spokane which underwent its catastrophic fire the very month he arrived. He immediately set out in what one observer called the "city of tents" to gather a few Germans together and preach to them in a small house. Though it was a humble beginning, fraught with financial difficulty (typical of most early Northwest missionary activity), a congregation was soon organized with the first installation of officers on September 1, 1889. The construction of a building was com-

Fig. 57. Reverend Henry H. Rieke. (H. H. Rieke)

Fig. 58. Evangelical Peace Lutheran Church in Tacoma, Washington founded in 1909. The building originally belonged to Zion Luthern Church (Missouri Synod) and was built in 1895.

Fig. 59. Christ Lutheran Church, Farmington, Washington founded in 1896.

pleted the following year and Emmanuel Church was dedicated on Easter Day, 1890.

Reverend Hein resigned his duties at Emmanuel in March, 1893 to devote his full energies to work among the English-speaking populace of the community. These labors reached fruition with the formation of the First English Evangelical Lutheran Church in Spokane on March 1, 1893.[38] About the time the financial panic of 1893-94 struck the Pacific Northwest, and in the decade the region took to fully recover, the district's pastors endeavored to enlarge their parishes. They did this despite the fact that their salaries were lowered, some receiving as little as fifteen dollars per month.[39]

During the late 1880s the need for additional men to work among the Germans in the Puget Sound area was growing and was answered by 1890. At this time pastors entering service with the Synod in Puget Sound included C. Lembke at Lake Bay, A. Krause in Tacoma's "New Addition", and L.H. Schuh who replaced Reverend Wolf at Trinity in Tacoma. Significantly, the contrast between the great poten-

191

tial of the entire Northwest District for the church and the acute lack of clergy did not fail to gain attention at the 1889 Diaspora Conference in Germany. The Reverend Dr. Borchard, who had visited the work in the Pacific Northwest, reported in an address to that body that:

> It is beyond all doubt, that the states along the Pacific Coast are of the greatest importance for the future of the United States and of the German Evangelical (Lutheran) Church. I therefore commend to your activity the mission work of the German Evangelical Church and school on the Pacific Ocean, especially the fruitful Washington Territory, West Oregon and California.[40]

Echoing Horace Greeley's adage, "Go West, young man," Pastor Schuh in Tacoma wrote, "Young preacher, go West" in a field report to the Synod in May, 1890 filled with hope and detailing the present needs of the district.[41] The response by several missionaries who journeyed West about this time is significant in that it contributed to the organization of an effective Joint Synod pastoral network among the Germans in the Northwest. This occurred at a time when many in the Synod were advocating a policy of retrenchment and consolidation in the more firmly established districts of the Midwest and East.[42] Reverend Schuh's article announced the recent arrival of Pastor C. Pitzler, who would soon be assigned to Fairfield, Washington and told of plans to place a man in Walla Walla.[43] It was Pastor C.F. Vollmer who responded to the call there in 1890 at Emmanuel Church, but was compelled to resign the following year due to tuberculosis and returned to the Midwest. The work in Walla Walla was carried on by Pastor A.F. Gillman from 1892-1895 who was in turn succeeded by Pastor A. Eberle from 1895-1899.[44]

The Schuh article also reported on the continuing activities of Pastor C. Lembke at Lake Bay and Reverend A. Krause, who was ministering to a mission of forty communicants in Tacoma. Within a year Pastors C. Haase and J. Willers arrived to serve congregations in Leber and Tacoma respectively. While citing Spokane, The Dalles, and Tacoma as the centers of the three principal fields of missionary activity, the area of roughly 3,000 square mile served by Pastor Rieke in southeastern Washington and northern Idaho did not escape Schuh's attention as he mentioned the district's intentions to place two additional men in openings there. Certainly the arduous tasks involved in serving such a field never escaped Reverend Rieke's thoughts but financial considerations had precluded the assignment of additional support there. Nevertheless, writing from Colfax on May 5, 1890 Pastor Rieke issued a call to

> Mr. Paul Groschupf of Afton, Minnesota as my assistant pastor in my congregation at Genesee and in my mission territory. I expect of you, dear Brother, that in assisting me in the discharge of our difficult but also precious vocation, you will faithfully stand at my side, so that, in every way, the honor of our God and our salvation and the souls entrusted to us, may be promoted....God give you grace to accept this call and follow it real soon![45]

Like Rieke, Paul Groschupf had emigrated from Germany to the United States after studying at the mission institute in Hermannsburg.

In an accompanying letter Pastor Rieke promised Groschupf free lodging in his home, a riding horse, and an annual salary of $250 while offering other arrangements if he chose to reside elsewhere.[46] The call was readily accepted; Groschupf moved to Cameron and was ordained to begin a prominent career as a missionary in Idaho and Washington. Later, he began his lengthy tenure as president of the district. One historian wrote the following graphic account of Groschupf's work:

> All the missionary's work had to be done on horseback for two reasons: the roads were very poor and the missionary's pocketbook was too slender for a buggy. (His horse was named Flora). Groschupf was a wild rider. Instead of opening gates, he with Flora jumped over them. He rode her through deep overflowing creeks, crossed the Clearwater River with her on a ferry, went down steep mountains and climbed them. The deep canyons were full of rattlesnakes. In order to escape their deadly bites, the rider had to lay his feet on the horse's neck and his back on the gown and books, which were tied in the saddle.[47]

Groschupf was called to Emmanuel Church in Spokane in 1895 and served faithfully there until his death in 1924.

It soon became clear to the Joint Synod that activities in the vast Northwest District were becoming too complicated to be dealt with as a single home mission field. For this reason the district was divided in 1890 into the Minnesota, Wisconsin, Kansas-Nebraska, Texas, and Pacific Districts.[48] This latter district convened for the first time from April 23-29, 1891 at Pastor Schuh's Trinity Lutheran Church in Tacoma.

One of the first orders of business was to legitimize the district's official name which, while it presumably would be called the Pacific District, was named the Washington District largely due to the difficulty for the German tongue in pronouncing the former term. Basing his text on I Corinthians 15:28, the newly formed district's senior pastor, Rev. F. N. Wolf, sounded the theme of the assembly in his address with the words: "The Lord hath done great things for us; whereof we are glad."

A large portion of the conference was dedicated to the delivery and discussion of the report by Pastor P.F. Hein entitled *"Das Missionwerk im fernen Nordwesten."* It detailed the current status of the work and outlined methods for future endeavors among Russian Germans and other immigrant groups in the region. The report also dealt with the three-fold problem that would reoccur throughout the pioneer period: the need for more self-sacrificing men, the lack of financial support, and the dangerous proselyting of the fraternal lodges and sects.[50] The entire district was composed of thirty-two congregations and mission points numbering 780 souls. The district was divided into an Eastern (Spokane) and Western (Tacoma) Conference with the 120th Longitude being the dividing line, roughly corresponding to the crest of the Cascade Mountains.

Pastor A. Horn was assigned the chairmanship of the Spokane Conference which met for the first time in Cameron, Idaho from November 17-19 in 1891. The train only went as far as Kendrick, Idaho at that time and the pastors were compelled to ride on horseback over a snowy mountain to Cameron, nearly getting lost in the process. Nevertheless they succeeded in assembling for the conference where they elected the resident Pastor, P. Groschupf, secretary and P.F. Hein, the conference president.[51] The second annual conference meeting was held in Spokane from October 25-27, 1892. Following the election of officers, the assembly adopted a resolution requesting the Home Mission Board to "send three men, respectively to La Grande and Palouse City...and if possibly the third one to the 'Big Bend County,' Washington. Thus the field is enlarging and the great missionary work advancing."[52]

The 1890s were also marked by slowly expanding missionary efforts in the Pacific Northwest by the Missouri Synod. At the beginning of the decade, seven Synod pastors functioned in the region, most west of the Cascades, and in December, 1890, Trinity Lutheran Church in Albina, Oregon was organized by Pastor J.H. Theiss in an area inhabited by many Volga Germans.[53] With the addition of only one man in 1891, Pastor C.J. Heuer, missionary efforts by the Synod were renewed east of the Cascades as Heuer located that year in Pendleton to serve the area. Moreover, his efforts took him to Endicott, Washington where he organized the Zion Evangelical Lutheran Church in 1891 among German and Volga German immigrants who had settled between Endicott and St. John, Washington. Candidate F. Schoknecht replaced Heuer the following year with the latter relocating to Sherwood, Oregon while Schoknecht shifted the center of his · mission work northward to Endicott. His goal was to serve the Volga German immigrants and others who were moving to Eastern Washington.[54] The Endicott congregation continued to grow and Schoknecht opened a parochial school there while establishing additional preaching points in the area until he moved to Minnesota in May, 1893.[55] Pastor F. Verwiebe began work in Spokane in 1893, but his responsibilities there prevented normal service to the Zion congregation and others in rural areas. As a result, many families in these areas transferred their memberships to established Joint Synod churches in Eastern Washington and Northern Idaho which numbered eleven by 1893.

Noting the change in Ohio's strategy, it soon became clear to Missouri Synod pastors in the Northern (Pacific) Conference that if effective organization and growth was to be achieved, a separate Synodical district was needed solely

195

for the Pacific Northwest. Such a proposal was submitted and adopted in April, 1899 at the St. Louis Delegate Convention. This led to the formation in August of the same year of the Oregon and Washington District. The district met that month for the first time with six lay delegates, nine pastors, and one teacher assembling at Zion in Portland. They elected as President Reverend H.A.C. Paul of St. Peter's Lutheran Church in Blooming, Oregon who in his sermon for the occasion challenged the district to "be ever conscious of its tremendous mission duties, and try to do justice to the obligations which this vast territory of these three states — Oregon, Washington and Idaho — places upon it."[56]

Mission work soon expanded to Northern Idaho as Candidate William Koss began ministering in 1900 to groups in the Camas Prairie at Grangeville, Denver, and Lowie.[57] By the time the 1901 district convention met, five new men had been added and services were being conducted on a regular basis in Odessa, Menno, and Yakima.[58] St. John's Lutheran Church had been founded in Spokane in 1900 after years of labor there by Pastor Verwiebe and the work among Volga Germans of Endicott was revived the same year as Pastor Heuer accepted a call there, replaced in 1902 by Pastor Schmelzer, who was then followed by Pastor H.A.C. Paul (1902-1906).[59]

Pastor Edward Doering continued to be one of the prime motivators of mission work for the Missouri Synod throughout his forty-year career in the Pacific Northwest. A meticulous chronicler, the following selection from a 1902 journal and letter indicates the extent of their work among the Russian Germans and others in the Big Bend country as well as the rivalry with the Joint Synod:

> February 8 — Saturday. Trip to Odessa, city of the Russians. Here almost everything is German. Our people live twelve miles south of here; they have founded a congregation; six members have joined, three have announced their intention of joining, still others want to come from the East. As soon as the Ohioans heard that a school was to be built, they began to hold their services nearby in a school house. Ohio is always right on the spot, they have their "pioneers" stationed everywhere. The Mission Board is certainly not familiar with the importance of this field. Therefore I shall describe it a bit. The so-called "Big Bend" is a district une-

qualed. The prairie extends about 150 miles long, 150 miles wide, and is covered partly with bunchgrass, partly with sage brush. Since people have discovered that the soil is exceptionally good for the raising of wheat the farmers are moving here from cold Minnesota and Dakota; yes, they are coming by the hundreds to establish homes here. Therefore, it is absolutely necessary that help be given to the congregation at Odessa to obtain a pastor who can gather and serve our people.[60]

Russian German settlement expanded westward along the recently completed route of the Great Northern Railroad and Doering decided to inspect this area as well. It is clear that the Missouri Synod had not been aware of the dynamic changes taking place there since the construction of the Crab Creek line in 1892. Doering was astonished to see how rapidly the small communities were progressing.

> February 10 — Monday. I rode westward to Wilson Creek. As I arrived there, I found half the town under water. The creek had overflowed; I rode out into the country on a boat, for which the brave boatman demanded his "nickel." I was told that a year ago only one hut stood here, now over fifty houses have been built, three hotels, stores, a bank, even a newspaper office, two schools, and the like. The roads are practically impassable, the snow is beginning to become soft, the "coulees" (ravines) are running full of snow water. On Tuesday I found an opportunity to ride in the direction of a German settlement. I rode along, but still had to walk two miles and then found the Germans. They moved here last fall from Minnesota, but are Evangelical and are being served every two weeks....
>
> Since there is now a vacancy at Endicott and the confirmation instruction which had already been begun should be concluded, I shall go there and finish it.
> Most respectfully,
>   Your humble servant of the Word,
>
>   (signed) Ed Doering[61]

Congregations of both Lutheran synods generally increased in size through the first decade of the twentieth century although problems resulting from lack of pastors continued to plague them and put tremendous strain on those who functioned in the Pacific Northwest. In the Washington District of the Joint Synod alone some forty pastors withdrew to other areas between 1891 and 1914.[62] The Joint Synod, however, was the largest of the six main Lutheran bodies in

County	Population			Total County Church Mbshp.	German Congregational (1910)	Lutheran (1916)[4]	
	Total[1]	GR[2]	%f.b.[3]			Ohio Synod	Synodical Con.
Adams	10,920	1,099	60	2,449	415	557	48
Whitman	33,280	798	30	9,645	107	399	37
Walla Walla	31,931	715	25	9,968	60	601	93
Lincoln	17,539	464	—	4,778	201	514	61
Grant	8,698	377	34	1,424	41	55	60

[1]U.S. Bureau of the Census, *1910 Abstract.*
[2]First and second generation Germans from Russia in 1920, see Sallet p. 123.
[3]Russian Germans as % of foreign born.
[4]U.S. Bureau of the Census, *Religious Bodies, 1916.*

TABLE III: POPULATION TOTALS AND DENOMINATIONAL MEMBERSHIPS IN SELECTED EASTERN WASHINGTON COUNTIES

the Pacific Northwest by 1916, with its Washington District composed of sixty congregations, twenty-three missions[63] and had an adult membership in the state of 4,461.[64] At the same time membership in the Synodical Conference in Washington, of which the Missouri Synod held the vast majority in 1916, numbered 2,740.[65] (Denominational memberships for Lutherans and Congregationalists in the Eastern Washington counties of heaviest Russian German settlement are indicated in Table III).

It has been said that the pioneer period of Lutheranism in the Pacific Northwest drew to a close with the outbreak of the World War I which suspended European immigration to the region.[66] The Bolshevik Revolution in 1917 further curtailed emigration from Russia of Volga Germans and ushered in a period of tragedy for those who remained. Conditions there would have worsened considerably had it not been for Northwest Russian Germans who undertook a massive famine relief campaign through their churches. It was a remarkable demonstration of the cooperative spirit which continued among Volga German groups throughout the United States and Canada.

In 1920 and 1921 catastrophic droughts struck southwestern Russia where the people refused to harvest their crops in protest of requisitions by the Communist authorities. The 1921 harvest was only 37 per cent of normal for the region and led to the great Russian famine of 1921-23.[67] News of the disaster soon reached Volga Germans living in the Pacific Northwest who united with others nationally in what Herbert Hoover, chairman of the American Relief Administration, termed "efficiency and devotion" to deliver hundreds of thousands from starvation.[68]

Between 1914 and 1921 the population in the German colonies on the Volga dramatically fell from 600,000 to 359,-000.[69] This was due to many factors including the Russian Civil War, starvation, executions, and some resettlement. Letters streamed to Volga Germans in the Northwest from their families in Russia begging for help. The following letter from the Peter Morasch family in Jagodnaja Poljana, Russia sent during the 1920s to relatives in Endicott, Washington was typical of the confused state of affairs.

> I will let you know that we are without parents. Where they are is unknown to us. Mother all this time was in Yakutsk (Siberia). But where they are now is known only to God....It (their assumed arrest) was a very bitter pain for us the children.
>
> ...Will you not take mercy on us because we are lost and without money? It is dear uncles, everything so high priced that rye flour costs 70 rubles per pood[70] and the potatoes, a sack is 40 rubles, so we cannot buy them. Will you not take pity on us because if not we will not be long on this earth. We have to put everything in the hands of God, what God does that is well done.[71]

Such correspondence evoked great sympathy and willingness to help on the part of Russian Germans in North America and when the Volga Relief Society was formed an effective network was established to channel funds to the areas of greatest need. News of the disastrous famine received widespread coverage in the Western press during the summer of 1921. At that time Mr. and Mrs. George Repp of Portland had been considering methods to aid the suffering Volga populace. Like hundreds of Volga Germans in Portland, the Repps were natives of the Volga colony of Norka. Discussing the various alternatives with John W. Miller, Mrs. Repp's brother, it was decided to organize a relief society and before a meeting was formally arranged, Miller cabled the following letter to American Relief Administration (ARA) on August 8, 1921:

> There are approximately fifteen hundred people in Portland that came from German colonies located in Russia near city of Saratov along Volga River. These people are anxious to help get food into that stricken district of Russia. They have received letters from relatives appealing for help. Will you be good enough to wire us how to proceed....There will be a mass meeting Thursday evening among our people and a regular relief committee organized for German speaking colonies in Russia....Have hopes extending work of this committee to other places where our people are located in California, Washington, Idaho, Montana, Colorado, Dakotas, Nebraska, Iowa, and Kansas. We figure that there are in the United States approximately a hundred thousand people interested in these German speaking colonies along the Volga River and that good work can be done with proper help from reliable source like yourselves. Would it be possible for us to send an American citizen of our people be endorsed by you or even sent by you as one of your workers so that he would have

proper protection.

John W. Miller[72]

The following day Miller received a telegram from Edgar Rickhard of the ARA expressing their willingness to channel contributions for relief work, although it would be confined to feeding children. Funds could not be designated for assistance in any particular locality in Russia until later. Encouraged by this response, the Repps and Miller held a public meeting attended by about one hundred people at Zion Congregational Church in Portland on August 11, 1921 and organized the Volga Relief Society.[73]

On August 18 a second meeting was held as interest spread and $6,075 were taken in pledges for relief to twenty different Volga German colonies. Plans were dicussed to form a national organization, and this was effectuated through the sending of a circular letter to German Congregational churches throughout the United States and Canada. Other denominations soon became involved in the program, principally Lutheran and Evangelical churches that had large Volga German memberships. The organizational meetings of the society in Portland particularly benefited from the advice of Congregational Pastors H. Hagelganz, George Zocher, and John H. Hopp, Reverend Peter Yost of the Brethren Church, and an Evangelical Church minister, Reverend Jacob Hergert.[74]

On August 21 permission was given to the society to send a delegate to Russia who would work with the ARA staff in their distribution program. George Repp was selected to go on what would become a great humanitarian venture. At the same meeting a strategy was planned to actively involve other Volga German communities. Reverend Zocher was sent to California and Reverend Hagelganz was assigned to Nebraska, Colorado, and Montana. A separate group was being formed in the Midwest, organized in Lincoln during September as the Central States Volga Relief Society which cooperated with the Portland group, and a third organization was established later in Denver, the Rocky Mountain States Volga Relief Society.

In September Pastor Hopp began traveling throughout

Eastern Washington in order to organize several branch societies of the Portland group. He met an enthusiastic response in Odessa where the work was spearheaded by Rev. J.H. Eckhardt. Both Volga and Black Sea Germans joined efforts through the next year in contributing the remarkable sum of $4,184.84, a total exceeded only by the cities of Portland, Fresno, and Denver. Additional meetings were held by Rev. Hopp in Ritzville, where the work was directed by Rev. Jacob Morach and William Thiel and in Dryden where Pastor John Reister of the Congregational Church was assisting in fund raising.

Branch societies were also organized in Endicott under the guidance of Rev. C.J. Wagner and in Walla Walla under the leadership of Pastor Paul Krumbein. Within three weeks of their receipt of Miller's original circular letter, $3,236.81 was received from these two groups. Additional support was given through the National Lutheran Council and the American Red Cross.[75] Local Ladies Aid auxiliaries in Lutheran churches in the Northwest and other denominations in the region initiated a massive campaign in the fall to send clothing to Volga German families in need. In October the Soviet authorities agreed to a program of Food Drafts suggested by Mr. Miller and others through which aid could be designated to specific families.

George Repp's arrival in the Volga German villages was heralded by great excitement, and he became referred to as the "father of our children" by the people. Despite the inevitable transportation delays caused by the Russian winter, the aid society nevertheless succeeded in regularly feeding 40,000 children by February, 1922.[76] The pastor in Alt-Messer, Rev. Edward Eichhorn, reported on the situation in his village on New Year's Day:

> The 1200 children who are now being fed in the American kitchens send their utmost sincere thanks for the food which they receive. Their parents, however, look into the year 1922 with fearful hearts, and can only pray that their lives will be spared. In the past year 800 people in Messer died of starvation and an additional 400 left for other sections where they hoped to find bread. Alt-Messer now contains 3600 inhabitants as compared with its former population of 5000. Our people live on mere scraps of

food; their clothing has been sold, and they lift their arms in
despair to an unmerciful heaven.

Eichhorn's letter also noted how inflation had caused soaring
food prices in Russia.

Prices are exorbitantly high; one pound of black bread costs
14,000 rubles; one pound of meat, 13,000 rubles; one pound of
fresh butter 50,000 rubles; one cow, 3,000,000 rubles; one pair of
oxen, 28,000,000 rubles, etc. These figures may give you some
idea of our present struggles for existence.[77]

Food Drafts remained the only way through which adults
could receive food and this system, introduced in October,
1921 was not always reliable at first. Some were drawn out in
January in Norka by several inhabitants who responded with
thanksgiving in the following note:

Although conditions in Norka get worse every day, we were
greatly encouraged last Thursday when ten sleighs of provisions
were brought to our village. Each of us received nine poods from
our relatives in America. Many families who were on the verge of
despair, have now been given new hope of being able to survive
until the next harvest. We wish to thank everyone who helped in
sending this food to us, and pray that God's richest blessings will
reward them for what they have done.[78]

During 1921 and 1922, the Volga Relief Societies contributed approximately $550,000 worth of food, clothing, and
other materials. Combined with the services rendered by the
National Lutheran Council and through various charitable
organzations for relief work to the Volga Germans, the total
figure amounted to over one million dollars.[79] An equal sum
was used in ARA relief work to aid Germans living in the
Black Sea region, Volynia, and elsewhere in Russia.[80] Praising the role of the Portland society, an official in the ARA
New York office wrote: "You may rest assured that not only
have no other communities of Germans equalled the efforts
of the Volga Relief Society due practically entirely to the activities of your Portland organization, but no other organization outside, of course, of the various members of the European Relief Council, of any race or religion has equalled
yours."[81]

With good crops assured for the 1922 harvest in July,
George Repp departed Russia for America. The following

November, the Portland, Lincoln, and Denver societies united to form the American Volga Relief Society which continued for several years, rendering service when needed until the Soviet government prevented further assistance. The society also served of great value to Volga Germans in the Pacific Northwest and throughout the nation as it facilitated communication and fellowship while perpetuating elements of their unique culture.

EPILOGUE

The late nineteenth century was characterized by the greatest westward migration of people in the history of the United States. Many individuals who had been effected by the Civil War were eager to move into the great expanse of the trans-Mississippi West at the conclusion of the conflict. Others who moved onto the "Great American Desert" came from abroad, from the many countries of the Old World. Some of these new immigrants were influenced by factors pushing them from their European homelands while others were affected by conditions in America which lured them to the land of promise. Millions of immigrants flooded to the United States, and they greatly influenced the course of American history. This was true of the many groups and successive waves of immigrants who traveled to this country to begin life anew. This certainly was the case for the Volga Germans.

Much of what had occurred in their past prepared the Volga Germans for their migration to and settlement in the United States. Their earlier move from Germany to Russia had prepared them well for their immigration to the American West. The Volga Germans had experienced the trauma of leaving their homeland, their families, and their identity with Germany. Despite the rigors of the move to the Volga region, they maintained as much as possible, their cultural identity as Germans. This factor contributed to the cohesiveness of the people, but it did not endear them to the Russians who were suspicious, if not envious, of the Germans. The Volga Germans had established colonies in Russia, and this pattern of settlement was used to good purpose by the people when they made the journey to America.

There were four major factors that resulted in the migration of the Volga Germans to the United States. True, there were those who traveled to the United States to seek adventure and be a part of the exaggerated glamor of the Western American experience. These individuals were very few in number, however, for the Volga Germans moved to the

205

United States for more practical reasons. Most immediate was the fear of being drafted into the Russian army, a fate that was so dreaded by the Volga Germans that they wanted to flee their homes and families to seek sanctuary in the United States. Economics was yet another reason for the migration of the people. It was difficult, many times impossible, for the Germans in the Volga region to purchase more land. As the years passed, the lands owned by the Germans had been divided time and again among the men. After successive generations of this process, the parcels were too small to make a good living. There was little hope that this trend would change in the later part of the nineteenth century. In fact, conditions for those Germans who remained in Russia would become worse, much worse.

Discrimination against the Germans in Russia grew in the nineteenth century, and it contributed significantly to the migration of the people from Europe to the United States. There were two forms of discrimination, one that affected all of the Germans in the Volga region and one that affected a large portion of those who left Russia for religious reasons. The form of discrimination that influenced all Russian Germans originated from an external force outside of the German colonies. It emerged from the native Russians and their government. The official Russian policy in dealing with the Germans evolved from paternal care to passive neglect and finally to one of aggressive Russification. In the mid-nineteenth century the Russian government decided to force their German colonists to acculturate and assimilate into Russian society. This change in governmental policy was most pronounced in the demand that the Germans educate their children in the Russian style which, of course, included the use of the Russian language, not the German.

In addition to discrimination resulting from the government, there were conditions within the German colonies that resulted in the discrimination of a portion of their own group. The internal conflict was religious in nature and emerged within the Lutheran Church. The Brotherhood, a splinter group within the Lutheran community, was formed as a result of doctrinal disagreements. Many of the first Volga

Germans who moved to the Midwest were members of the Brotherhood and they formed a separate denomination once they arrived in the United States — German Congregationalism. These two forms of discrimination were instrumental in the immigration of the Germans from Russia.

Another factor contributing to the migration of the Volga Germans, indeed many Europeans, were the huge and effective advertising campaigns that were launched to attract setlers to the United States. Steamship and railroad companies worked diligently to encourage large-scale European migration. The immigrants were extremely important to the transportation businesses of the United States. The Europeans purchased fares for the ocean crossing, tickets for their journey by rail once they had arrived, and necessities of life while they were in transit. Moreover, the immigrants purchased land owned by the railroad companies.

The transportation companies realized that once the immigrants had settled, they would use their systems as a means to transport their products to foreign and domestic outlets. The railroads had much to gain in the short and long term, from the advertising campaigns, so they established bureaus of immigration and land departments. They bombarded Europe with advertisements, all of which made the American West appear to be as attractive as Heaven itself. The Volga Germans read about the West in their newspaper where American companies had taken out space to popularize the West and promote immigration. The Volga Germans and other Europeans conjured up an image of the West from viewing the many picturesque posters and reading the mass of colorful prose printed in the promotional brochures produced by the transportation companies. By the time the Germans began their journey to America, they were convinced that the American West was a Garden of Eden, a virtual "land of milk and honey."

The Volga Germans were like other immigrants in many ways. Despite their eagerness to venture across the sea to the New World, it was not an easy thing to do. There were many hardships and heartaches to endure. They left their home on the Volga, never to return, and they weathered a difficult passage across the ocean which produced anxiety, stress, and doubt. Sickness was common aboard ship, and some immigrants, including children, died on the journey to the United States. Fear and apprehension emerged within the minds of the Volga Germans. They were going to a new country where they had to deal with foreign people who spoke a foreign tongue. They kept their spirit by leaning on one another and maintaining their religious faith. Fortunately for many groups of Volga Germans, they received immediate help as soon as they arrived. They were met at the docks by representatives of the immigration companies who could speak English as well as German. Nevertheless, the Volga Germans, like all of the immigrants, had to face the immigration officials of the United States, not a pleasant task at all. When they had completed these procedures, they traveled through the hectic city of New York and began their journey overland to their new far-off homes in the American West.

While the Volga Germans shared these experiences with other immigrants of the era, they were unique in some ways. For one, many moved to America and onto the Great Plains as colonial groups. Most immigrants, whether they were Irish, Italian, Polish, etc., traveled to the United States as individuals, not as colonies. The Volga Germans differed greatly then in this respect. Not only did they travel as a unified body, a colony, but they came to America with a plan of how they would immigrate, settle, and make a living. The Volga Germans were of rural origin, not urban, and therefore they planned even before departing to settle on farms in the trans-Mississippi West. This was important not only to their immediate well being, but to their image as recent immigrants to America. They were very much unlike many immigrants who became associated with the urban problems of the United States. The Volga Germans never planned to remain in the industrial cities of the East and thus were spared the ugly image that nativistic Americans had toward some of the recent arrivals. The Volga Germans did not suffer from the ills related to a miserable life in the urban slums and they did not have to live with the image of being creators of America's ghettos. In addition, they did not suffer religious persecution known to Catholics and Jews who remained in the cities.

The international phenomenon of immigration to the United States brought the Volga Germans to the shores of their chosen country. Once they arrived, they began their journey overland by railroad to farmlands on the Great Plains. As colonies they moved to Kansas and Nebraska, which years before their arrival had been part of the large Indian Territory. There were Indians residing in Kansas and Nebraska after the Civil War, but the Volga Germans had little contact with them. The newcomers spent the bulk of their time trying to eke out a living on the prairies of American's heartland. There were many problems to overcome by the new settlers living in the region. Most of them remained in spite of the prolonged droughts, the harsh winters, the destructive grasshoppers. A few returned to Russia. Other Volga German groups decided to pick up their roots once again and move west because of the promise of new opportunity in that region. Their experiences, lessons they learned when things did not turn out the way they had expected, helped them immensely when they resettled in the Pacific Northwest.

Like so many other immigrants, the Volga Germans were lured to new lands farther west as a result of advertising. They moved to the Pacific Northwest, in large measure, because of the efforts of the Northern Pacific Railroad and its subsidiary organizations. The Northern Pacific Railroad encouraged immigration to the Northwest by paying the fares of members of an immigrant group interested in making an exploring expedition to the region. This technique worked very well for the transportation companies, and once the representatives of the Volga Germans saw the Columbia Plain, they were convinced that they could in fact transform the region into a "land of milk and honey." With favorable reports of the area in hand, the Volga Germans began their move to the isolated regions of the "New Northwest." Traveling by wagon roads and by steel rails, they migrated overland to the greater Northwest. They would make their homes in this unique region of the United States, and they would offer much to the overall economic development of the Pacific Northwest.

The settlement of Volga Germans on the great Columbia Plain was more than a story of one "farmer's frontier." The Volga Germans were part of a much larger settlement pattern in the United States and the American West. They peopled an area that had once been the sole domain of Indians who had hunted and gathered on the lands that were to be cultivated by those who had only recently arrived in the "New World."

By the time the Volga Germans had arrived in the Northwest, the government had forced the first Americans onto reservations and had liquidated their title to the vast hills and prairies. The Indians had lived in harmony with the land, and they had not, for the most part, farmed. For hundreds of years the land had remained virtually untouched by the hands of man. The Volga Germans, however, and other white immigrants in the region were different from the Indians. They had come to till the soil, to work the land, and to produce a livelihood from farming.

Volga German settlement of the Pacific Northwest significantly changed the region. The face of the land itself changed dramatically as the farmers turned the soil, planted their crops, and harvested their produce. Economics therefore changed in a land that had once been dominated by the Indian trade, fishing, and livestock grazing. Farming became a major factor in the Northwest during the late nineteenth century, and it did so, in part, because of the work performed by the Volga Germans. The presence of Volga Germans in the Northwest changed the social fabric of the region. They and other immigrants created a patchwork of newcomers in the Northwest. Although the Volga Germans were quick to understand the social structure and cultural elements of the larger society, they held steadfastly to some of their customs, teachings, and general techniques of their past lifeway. Some of them held onto the cultural heritage of the Volga Germans, a heritage that was centuries old and had emerged through both the German and Russian experiences. This was particularly apparent in their religion. Some of the doctrine had changed, but the role of the church in society

210

had not changed. Religion and the church was the center of life in the Volga German community. The church was involved in every aspect of Volga German life. Political, social, and cultural matters were discussed and handled in and through the church. Thus, the church was an institution within Volga German society that remained significant once the immigrants had moved to the United States.

Nowhere is the lasting importance of the Volga Germans seen better than in the realm of economics. Farming in the region has been a continuous crucial economic factor in the Pacific Northwest, indeed the world. Volga Germans contributed much to the growth and development of agriculture in the region that otherwise would have suffered more severely from soil depletion. They introduced new methods of soil fertilization and crop rotation. They turned the dry prairies of the Columbia Basin into productive fields by irrigating their crops. In many ways the Volga Germans contributed to the economic development of the Northwest.

The Volga Germans were much more than settlers and they contributed a great deal to the settlement of the Pacific Northwest. They were part of a national movement to fill up the land and make it productive. In so doing, the Volga Germans played an important role in the nation's destiny. Like the business community of the East, the farmers of the West provided the vehicle through which the United States emerged as a world power in the early twentieth century. The Volga Germans were a part of all of this, and their significance to American History in general and the American West in particular, too long unappreciated, was indeed great.

NOTES

INTRODUCTION

1. Will Durant, *The Reformation: A History of European Civilization from Wyclif to Calvin, 1300-1564* (New York: Simon and Schuster, 1957), p. 380.

2. Fred Koch, *The Volga Germans: In Russia and the Americas, from 1763 to the Present* (University Park: Pennsylvania State University Press, 1977), p. 5.

3. The calculated decrease in Germany's population during the war was from 21,000,000 to 13,500,000. Hundreds of villages were left totally unoccupied, thousands of acres in the surrounding fields were left uncultivated and the peasants were reduced to eating rats and grass, some even resorting to cannibalism.

4. Koch, p. 5

5. Hattie Plum Williams, *The Czar's Germans: With Particular Reference to the Volga Germans* (Lincoln, Nebraska: A.H.S.G.R., 1975), p. 6.

6. Nicholas V. Riasonovsky, *A History of Russia* (New York: Oxford University Press, 1969), p. 275.

7. Wilhelm Würz, "Wie Jagodnaja Poljana gegründet wurde," *Heimatbuch der Deutschen aus Russland,* (1962), p. 65.

8. "Bericht der Regierung zu Giessen und den Landgrafen," (April 4, 1767), *Acten des Geheimen Staats-Archivs, XI,* Abtheilung, Convolut I, in the Hessian State Archives, Darmstadt, West Germany, quoted in Williams, p. 20.

9. Karl Esselborn, "Die Auswanderung von Hessen nach Russland," *Heimat im Bild,* (1926), p. 84.

10. Emigration from southern Germany at this time was not limited to North America and Russia, rather many also settled in Brazil, Algeria and elsewhere in Europe. See Ernst Wagner, "Auswanderung aus Hessen," *Ausland-deutschtum und evangelischen Kirche Jahrbuch,* (1938).

11. Cited in Grigorii G. Pissarevskii, *Iz istorii inostrannoi kolonizatsii v rossi v XXIII v.* (Po neizdannym arkivnym dokumentam), (Moskva: A.I. Snegrirevyi, 1909), p. 180. *(History of Foreign Colonization in Russia in the Eighteenth Century. Based on Unpublished Archive Documents).*

CHAPTER I

1. This program is detailed in Pissarevskii, pp. 38-45.

2. Pissarevskii, p. 45.

3. A "German Suburb" in Moscow developed as early as the sixteenth century following the settlement there of a number of German craftsmen and teachers under the reign of Ivan the Terrible (1533-84). His efforts to

modernize the country through such programs were not continued by the early Romanov commercial ties to western Europe.

4. Karl Stumpp, *The German Russians: Two Centuries of Pioneering,* (Bonn, West Germany: Atlantic Forum, 1967), p. 6.

5. Adam Giesinger, *From Catherine to Khrushchev: The Sory of Russia's Germans,* (Battleford, Saskatchewan: Marian Press, 1974), p. 4

6. Pissarevskii, p. 48.

7. Gladys Scott Thomson, *Catherine the Great and the Expansion of Russia,* (New York: Collier Books, 1965), p. 119.

8. George J. Eisenach, *Pietism and the Russian Germans in the United States,* (Berne, Indiana: The Berne Publishers, 1948), p.17.

9. Pissarevskii, p. 45

10. *Ibid.,* p. 46

11. *Ibid.*

12. *Ibid.*

13. In this manifesto and later legislation directing the immigration program, Jews were forbidden to colonize in the country.

14. Pissarevskii, p. 48.

15. *Ibid.*

16. Williams, p. 38.

17. Pissarevskii, p. 49.

18. Russia, *Polnoe Sobranie Zakonov Rossiiskoi Imperii,* Vol. XVI, No. 11,800 (St. Petersburg, 1649-1916). *(Collection of Laws of the Russian Empire,* in the Hoover institution Library at Stanford University, Stanford, California).

19. Giesinger, p. 5.

20. *Ibid.*

21. Pissarevskii, p. 52.

22. David G. Rempel, "The Mennonite Commonwealth in Russia: A Sketch of its Founding and Endurance, 1789-1919," *Mennonite Quarterly Review, XLVII* (October, 1973), p. 11.

23. Pissarevskii, p. 51.

24. Giesinger, p. 9.

25. Williams, p. 43.

26. *Ibid.,* p. 45.

27. The perils of this journey are described in Gottlieb Bauer, *Geschichte dor Deutschen in Den Wolgakolonien* (Saratov, 1907), p. 19 and Gottlieb Beratz, *Die deutschen Kolonien an der Unteren Wolga,* (Saratov: H. Schellhorn u. Co., 1915), pp. 41-42.

28. These French recruiters, most of whom proved to be unscrupulous businessmen, included men named Beauregard, DeBoffe, LeRoy, Monjou,

Pictet, and Precourt.

29. Koch, p. 7.

30. While all aspects of Simolin's program were not always above reproach, there developed an intense rivalry between the two recruiting agencies as the Frenchmen were often accused of fraudulent business practices. For a fuller explanation see Pissarevskii, Appendix 17.

31. "Berichte des pruessischen Gesandten in Russland an Koenig Friederich II, 1766," quoted in Williams, p. 78.

32. "Schreiben der Churfuerstl. Mainzischen Regierung an die Fuerstl. Hessische wegen gemein schaftlicher Massregeln gegen fremde Werber," Mainz, February 7, 1766, found in the Hessen State Archives, Darmstadt, West Germany.

33. Esselborn, p. 84.

34. Williams, pp. 79-80.

35. Ibid., p. 84.

36. Pissarevskii, p. 148.

37. Letter from the government in Giessen to Ludwig VIII, Landgrave of Hessen-Darmstadt, quoted in Esselborn, p. 88.

38. Ernst Wagner, "Auswanderung aus Hessen," Auslanddeutschtum und evangelischen Kirche Jahrbuch, (1938), pp. 24-33.

39. Pissarevskii, Appendix 14.

40. Ibid.

41. Pissarevskii, p. 169.

42. As the equivalent of the foreign minister, the chancellorship was left vacant during most of Catherine's reign as she preferred to assume the responsibility herself, allowing vice-chancellors to execute her wishes although she was influenced to a great degree by various court favorites.

43. Pissarevskii, p. 168.

44. Ibid., p. 148.

45. Ibid., pp. 148-49.

46. From Tagebuch eines Schlitzer Bauern namens Adolf Weissbeck, in Arthur and Cleora Flegel, "Research in Hesse," A.H.S.G.R. Work Paper, No. 13 (December, 1973), pp. 24-25.

47. Georg Kromm, "Die deutschen Ansiedler an der Wolga," Schottener Kreisblatt, No. 15 (February 22, 1920), pp. 1-3.

48. Williams, p. 81.

49. Ibid.

50. Wagner, pp. 23-33.

51. Würz, p. 67. Special bonuses were given to families under the liberal terms of settlement.

52. Pissarevskii, p. 149.

53. Estimates given by Bauer and Beratz. Pissarevskii recorded 22,800 original German colonists to the Volga while Bonwetch suggested a figure of 25,000 was more accurate. Pallas in *Reisen durch verschiedene Provinzen des russichen Reiches in den Jahren 1768-1774* (St. Petersburg, 1771-76) put the number at about 29,000. The first census of the German Volga colonies was taken in 1769 under Count Orlov of the Guardianship Chancery, indicating a population then of 23,109 (10,894 in crown colonies and 12,215 in propietory with 137 allowed to settle in Saratov).

54. In addition a colony of Moravian Brethren from Herrnhut was established on the Volga at Sarepta, about 200 families founded four colonies in the province of St. Petersburg and 742 Germans from the area of Frankfurt a.M. settled in the Chernigov province.

55. Williams, p. 99. One of the original 104 colonies was settled by French colonists.

56. Williams, p. 87.

57. Pissarevskii, p. 117.

58. Other than colonization in the Josefstal, Fischerdorf and Jamberg districts near the Dneper River by Germans in 1780 and of Mennonites from Danzig and West Prussia to the Chortitza area from 1789-90, foreign settlement in Russia was suspended until 1804 when renewed efforts begun by Alexander I brought thousands of German settlers to the Black Sea region and later to the Caucasus. Mennonites came to Samara beginning in 1853 when they founded Köppenthal.

CHAPTER II

1. Christian G. Züge, *Der russiche Kolonist, I* (Zeitz und Naumberg: Wilhelm Webel, 1802), p. 49.

2. Williams, p. 107

3. Beratz, p. 45.

4. Giesinger, p. 11.

5. Williams, p. 109.

6. Beratz, p. 53.

7. Emma D. Swabenland, "German-Russians on the Volga and in the United States" (Unpublished Master's Thesis, University of Colorado, 1929), p. 17.

8. Demographic data on these villages is indicated in the following table (from Pissarevskii, pp. 74-83 and Karl Stumpp, *The Emigration from Germany to Russia in the Years 1763 to 1862,* (Tübingen, West Germany: by the author), pp. 67-77):

Colony	1769	1772	1912	1926
Balzer	410	479	11,110	11,556
Frank	425	525	11,557	5,191
Hussenbach	438	525	8,080	6,623
Jagodnaja Poljana	312	402	8,845	15,000*
Kolb	107	143	3,800	2,823
Messer	329	397	5,295	3,575
Norka	772	957	14,236	7,210
Walter	382	431	6.660	2,739
Warenburg	524	579	8,312	4,754

*The district population, consisting also of residents in Pobotschnoje and Neu Straub. Stumpp also provides a list of the original immigrants who founded the colonies of Jagodnaja Poljana and Balzer, pp. 77-81.

9. Züge, pp. 143-44.

10. Kratzke was located on the Karamysh. See Williams, p. 110, for a brief discussion on the disputed location.

11. Kromm also quotes a Saratov document which indicates the colony was founded on September 16, 1767. See George Kromm, *Einwanderliste von Jagodnaja Poljana* (aus Hessen). At the Volgelsberg Museum in Schotten, West Germany, reprinted in Esselborn, pp. 91-92.

12. Würz, p. 66.

13. Kromm, "Die deutschen Ainsiedler an der Wolga," *Schottener Kreisblatt,* (February 22, 1910), p. 2.

14. Koch, p. 25 and Mrs. Catherine Luft, private interviews, Sheboygan, Wisconsin. June 15-19, 1977.

15. Johannes Schleuning, *Die deutschen Kolonien im Wolgagebiet,* (Berlin, 1919), p. 20.

16. David Schmidt, *Studien über die Geschichte der Wolgadeutschen* (Polrowsk, ASSR der Wolgadeutschen: Zentral-Völker-Verlag, 1930), pp. 128-31, 138.

17. "The Years of Want".

18. Beratz, pp. 178-201.

19. Bauer, p. 105.

20. Esselborn, p. 92. Beideck's favorable location near the west bank of the Volga River and its early well supervised founding in 1764 may help explain the optimistic report.

21. Kromm, "Die deutschen Ansiedler an der Wolga," *Schottener Kreisblatt,* (February 25, 1910), p. 1.

22. Koch, p. 99.

23. The entire story of Stärkel's experience while captive was recorded

by Johannes Stärkel in "Johann Wilhelm Stärkel aus Norka unter der Fahne Pugaschews," *Friedensbote,* (November, 1910), pp. 85-88.

24. Bauer, p. 47.

25. *Ibid.,* p. 48.

26. Koch, p. 29.

27. *Ibid.,* p. 33.

28. Williams, p. 146.

29. Jacob Volz, *Historical Review of the Balzerer* (York, Nebraska, 1938), p. 4.

30. Schleuning, p. 11.

31. Conrad Blumenschein, oral interviews, St. John, Washington, May 6 and 13, 1980.

32. Koch, p. 55.

33. Blumenschein interviews.

34. Koch, p. 183.

35. *Ibid.,* p. 78 and Henry Litzenberger, oral interviews, Deer Park, Washington, May 4, 1980.

36. Koch, p. 77.

37. Blumenschein interviews.

38. Koch, pp. 185-186 and Blumenschein interviews.

39. Elizabeth Kromm, oral interview, LaCrosse, Washington, June 10, 1979.

40. Koch, p. 58.

41. Mrs. C.P. Morasch, oral interview, Endicott, Washington, April 23, 1971 and Susan M. Yungman, *Faith of Our Fathers* (by the author, 1972), p. 9.

42. Mr. and Mrs. John Schierman, oral interview, Vulcan, Alberta, July 2, 1977.

43. Elizabeth Kromm, oral interview, LaCrosse, Washington, June 10, 1979.

44. August Markel, oral interview, Endicott, Washington, June 19, 1970 and Blumenschein interviews.

45. Luft interviews.

46. Mrs. A.P. Morasch, oral interview, Endicott, Washington, March 4, 1980.

47. Alec Reich, oral interview, Endicott, Washington, April 2, 1969.

48. Blumenschein interviews.

49. Henry Litzenberger, oral interview, Deer Park, Washington, May 4, 1980.

50. Koch, p. 190.

51. Koch, pp. 68-69, quoting statistics given by Bonwetsch, Pallas and Beratz.

52. Aleksandr Avgustovich Klaus, *Nashii Kolonii: Opyty materialy po isotorii i statistike inostrannoi kolonizatsii v rossi* (St. Petersburg: Tipografiia V.V. Nusval't, 1869), pp. 190-95. *(Our Colonies: The Lessons of Materials Based on the History and Statistics of Foreign Colonization in Russia).*

53. Giesinger, p. 54.

54. From *mirskoi skhod,* the "village assembly" of the Russian peasant commune.

55. Klaus, pp. 189-195.

56. Blumenschein interviews.

57. George J. Eisenach, *Das religiöse Leben unter den Russland-deutschen in Russland und America* (Marburg an der Lahn, West Germany: Buchdruckerei Hermann Rathmann, 1950), Appendix I, pp. 214-16.

58. Betty Scott, unpublished papers, Mission, Kansas.

59. Henry Litzenberger, oral interview, Deer Park, Washington, May 4, 1980.

60. Grigorii G. Pissarevskii, *Vnutrennoi rasporiadok v koloniiakh povolzh'ia pri Ekaterine II.* (Varshava: Tipografiia varshavskago uchebnogo okruga, 1914), p. 10. *(Internal Order in the Volga Colonies during the Reign of Catherine II).*

61. Bauer, p. 64. These debts had been incurred largely through loans for home construction and operating expenses at the time of settlement. The slow recovery from the early period of drought and corruption in the collection of crown taxes delayed final liquidation of the debt until the 1840s, after a special investigation had been made into the matter.

62. Rempel, p. 58.

63. Beratz, p. 104.

64. Rempel, p. 58.

65. *Ibid.*

66. *Ibid.,* p. 63.

67. Koch, p. 93.

68. Giesinger, pp. 155-56. For an extensive treatment of the history of Lutheranism throughout the Russian and Soviet periods, see Edgar C. Duin, *Lutheranism under the Tsars and Soviets,* 2 Vols. (Ann Arbor, Michigan: University Microfilms, 1975).

69. *Ibid.,* p. 157.

70. *Ibid.,* p. 405. For a complete listing of the pastorates for each Volga German colony see Karl Stumpp, "Verzeichnis der ev. Pastoren in den deutschen und gemischten — vor allem in Städten — Kirchenspielen in Russland bzw. der Sowejetunion, ohne Baltikum und Polen," *Heimatbuch der Deutschen aus Russland,* (1969/72), pp. 276-389.

71. Eisenach, *Pietism and the Russian Germans...,* p. 40. For a full dis-

cussion of the activities of some of these missionaries in the Volga colonies, see Eisenach, chapter 3.

72. *Ibid.,* p. 39.

73. *Ibid.,* p. 40.

74. Giesinger, p. 161.

75. Eisenach, *Pietism and the Russian Germans...,* p. 41.

76. This popular collection of 823 hymns is still in use in Lutheran congregations in the Soviet Union.

77. Koch, p. 147.

78. For catechetical instruction the Lutheran Consistory allowed Reformed colony schools use of Rogue's Catechism, see *Schul- und Küster-Schulmeister Instruction in der evangelischen Kolonien des Saratovschen und Samaraschen Gouvernments,* (Moskva: Moskovischen Evangelischen Lutherischen Consistorio), undated.

79. Koch, p. 123.

80. Timothy Kloberdanz, "Funerary Beliefs and Customs of the Germans from Russia," *A.H.S.G.R. Work Paper,* No. 20 (Spring, 1976), p. 65.

81. Koch, pp. 154-55.

82. Giesinger, p. 173.

83. Eisenach, *Pietism and the Russian Germans...,* p. 66. This book gives a complete study on the origins and development of the German Russian pietistic movement.

84. *Ibid.,* p. 65 and Catherine Luft, Private interview, Sheboygan, Wisconsin, June 19, 1977.

85. *Ibid.,* pp. 67-68.

86. *Ibid.,* pp. 69-70.

87. Koch, p. 205.

88. Eisenach, *Pietism and the Russian Germans...,* p. 71.

89. Emma S. Haynes, "Researching in the National Archives," *A.H.S.G.R. Journal,* II, No. 1 (Spring, 1979), p. 4.

90. George Burgdorff, *Erlebnisse als Missionar oder Reiseprediger in Russland* (Hillsboro, Kansas: M.B. Publishing House, 1924), pp. 93, 151.

CHAPTER III

1. Bauer, p. 163.

2. Harm Scholommer, "Inland Empire Russia Germans," *The Pacific Northwesterner, VIII* (Fall, 1964), p. 60.

3. It was argued by some government authorities that the terms "century" and "forever" were synonymous in vernacular use during the time of Catherine II's reign. See Koch, p. 199.

4. Harry G. Scholz, "The German Colonists of Russia: The Repeal of

Russia's Law of the Colonists in 1871 and its effect on the German Colonist Population," (Unpublished Master's Thesis, Chapman College, Orange, California, 1969), p. 29. Several Mennonite delegations journeyed to St. Petersburg from 1871 to 1874 requesting continued exemption on religious grounds but met with little success until 1875 when conditional exemptions were allowed. See Rempel, p. 80. The complete text of the 1871 Ukase is found in: Russia, *Polnoe Sobranie Zakonov Rossiiskoi Imperii,* Vol. XLVI, No. 49, 705. (St. Petersburg, 1649-1916).

5. Rempel, pp. 78-79.

6. Giesinger, p. 227.

7. Scholz, pp. 37-38.

8. For a discussion of this earlier migration see Williams, pp. 180-181.

9. Williams, p. 189.

10. Koch, p. 205.

11. Emma S. Haynes, "Germans from Russia in American History and Literature," *A.H.S.G.R. Work Paper,* No. 15 (September, 1974), pp. 11-13.

12. Koch, pp. 206-207.

13. Bonwetsch, p. 114.

14. Scholz, p. 40.

15. Bonwetsch, p. 109.

16. Norman E. Saul, "The Arrival of the Germans from Russia: A Centennial Perspective," *A.H.S.G.R. Work Paper,* No. 21 (Fall, 1976), pp. 4-5.

17. Marcus Lee Hansen, *The Immigrant in American History* (Cambridge: Harvard University Press, 1940), p. 72. Timber cultures provided a quarter-section grant to any settler who planted 40 acres of trees although this was reduced to 10 acres in 1878. One could obtain title to 640 acres at $1.25 per acre under the terms of the Desert Land Act if it was placed under irrigation within three years of the filing date.

18. Norman Saul, "The Migration of Russian-Germans to Kansas," *Kansas Historical Quarterly, XL,* No. 1 (Spring, 1974), pp. 50-53.

19. *Hayes City Sentinal,* August 16, 1876.

20. *Topeka Daily Blade,* December 13, 1875.

21. *S.S. Ohio* Manifest (to Baltimore, November 23, 1875).

22. *S.S. City of Montreal* Manifest (to New York, January 6, 1876). This group of nearly 200 Volga Germans was under the leadership of Peter Ekkert, a Mennonite missionary.

23. Saul, "The Arrival of the Germans from Russia: A centennial Perspective," p. 7.

24. The terms "Kansas colony" and "Nebraska colony" are to be interpreted in the broader sense of the terms as it was from the general areas of Rush and Barton County, Kansas and Hitchcock County, Nebraska that Volga German immigration to the Pacific Northwest began.

25. *S.S. Mosel* Passenger List (to New York, October 24, 1876). The spelling of many Volga German names was altered after their arrival; Scheuermann to Schierman, Brach to Brack, Pfaffenroth to Poffenroth, etc.

26. From Peter Brack's autobiography, typescript copy, sent to Richard Scheuerman with letter from Laurin P. Wilhelm, Laurence, Kansas, April 27, 1974.

27. Leta Ochs, scrapbook clippings, Endicott, Washington.

28. Grace Lillian Ochs, *Up From the Volga: The Story of the Ochs Family* (Nashville: Southern Publishing Company, 1969), p. 29.

29. Mrs. Elizabeth Repp, private interview, Endicott, Washington, April 1, 1971.

30. Russel *Record,* December 7, 1876.

31. Richard Sallet, *German-Russian Settlements in the United States* (Fargo: North Dakota Institute for Regional Studies, 1974), translated by LaVern J. Rippley and Armand Bauer, pp. 23-24.

32. Johann Hoezler, "The Earliest Volga Germans in Sutton, Nebraska and a Portion of their History," *A.H.S.G.R. Work Paper,* No. 16 (December, 1974), translated by Arthur Flegel, p. 16.

33. Williams, p. 177.

34. Saul, "The Arrival of the Germans from Russia: A Centennial Perspective," p. 5.

35. *The London Times,* February 1, 1876.

36. The names of these Volga German settlers appear in Hoezler, pp. 16-17.

37. *S.S. Donau* Manifest (to New York, August 5, 1876), and Roy Oestrich, unpublished papers, Ritzville, Washington. Scheibel was originally from the village of Messer.

38. Pauline B. Dudek, "Further Notes on the Wagon Train from Nebraska to Washington," *A.H.S.G.R. Journal,* II, No. 3 (Winter, 1979), p. 44.

39. *S.S. Wieland* Passenger List (to New York, June 5, 1878).

40. For settlement conditions in this area, see Frederick C. Luebke, *Immigrants and Politics: The Germans of Nebraska, 1880-1900* (Lincoln: University of Nebraska Press, 1969).

41. Roy Oestrich, unpublished papers, Dudek, p. 45.

42. *Endicott Index,* November 29, 1935.

43. Dave Schierman, private interview, Walla Walla, Washington, July 9, 1972.

44. Enoch A. Bryan, *Orient Meets Occident: The Advent of the Railways to the Pacific Northwest* (Pullman, Washington: The Student Book Corporation, 1936), pp. 141-142.

221

CHAPTER IV

1. Henry Villard, *The Early History of Transportation in Oregon* (Eugene: University of Oregon Press, 1944,), pp. 37-38.

2. *Ibid.,* p. 40.

3. *Ibid.,* p. 43.

4. *Ibid.,* p. 50.

5. *Ibid.,* p. 65.

6. *Ibid.*

7. *Bryan, p. 141.*

8. *Ibid.,* p. 109.

9. The Northern Pacific constructed a short track between Ainsworth and Wallula in order to reach the coast on the Oregon Railway and Navigation Company line.

10. Bryan, p. 144.

11. Villard, p. 89.

12. David Lavender, *Land of Giants: The Drive to the Pacific Northwest, 1740-1940* (Garden City, New York: Doubleday and Company, 1958), p. 380.

13. Bryan, p. 148.

14. *Forty-fifth Annual Reunion of the Association of the Graduates of the United States Military Academy at New York, June 12th, 1914* (Saginaw, Michigan: Seeman and Peters, Inc., 1914), pp. 105-110 and Mrs. Hazel (Tannatt) Engelland, private interview, Lacey, Washington, April 20, 1978.

15. Villard, p. 85.

16. James B. Hedges, *Henry Villard and the Railways of the Northwest* (New Haven: Yale University Press, 1930), p. 127.

17. Bryan, pp. 149-51.

18. Villard, p. 97.

19. Ochs, p. 26, Mrs. Karl L. Scheuerman, private interview, Endicott, Washington, June 8, 1975 and Mrs. Leta Ochs, private interview, Endicott, Washington, April 23, 1971, 1883 Territorial Census Records, Whitman County, Washington Territory and Anna Weitz file.

20. Ochs, p. 36-38.

21. Letter, R.W. Mitchell, Colfax, W.T. to Tannatt, Portland, Oregon, May 10, 1881.

22. Letter, Tannatt, Dayton, W.T. to Villard, May 10, 1881.

23. Notation by Tannatt on Mitchell letter, forwarded to Villard, May 11, 1881.

24. Letter, Carl Brobst, interpreter at Culbertson, Hitchcock County, Nebraska to J.E. Shepherd, Oregon Railway and Navigation Company, San Francisco, California, May 10, 1880; quoted in Hedges, p. 124.

25. Roy Oestreich file.

26. *Ritzville Journal-Times,* "Adams County Pioneer Edition," September 15, 1949; Ruth J. Thiel, "Memories of my Father," unpublished typescript and Roy Oestreich file.

27. *Ritzville Journal-Times,* "Adams County Pioneer Edition," September 15, 1949, pp. 1-3. Evidence suggests that John H. Koch and Henry H. Rehn were among the group that went to Portland. See Dudek, p. 45.

28. Roy Oestreich file. Ritz was originally from Pennsylvania, born in Lancaster County in 1827. He came west during the California gold rush but in 1850 moved to Winchester Bay, Oregon after reading about strikes along the Umpqua River. Instead, all he found were Indians and dense forests so he turned to trapping. He went north to Canada's Fraser River gold district in 1858. Four years later he opened a tree nursery in Walla Walla which developed into a profitable enterprise and later acquired extensive land holdings. He died in 1889.

CHAPTER V

1. Richard D. Scheuerman, "Patterns of Settlement in the Palouse Country, 1860-1915" (Unpublished Manuscript, 1980), p. 8.

2. Donald W. Meinig, *The Great Columbia Plain: A Historical Geography, 1805-1910* (Seattle: University of Washington Press, 1968), p. 245.

3. *Ibid.,* pp. 238, 245.

4. Bryan, p. 161.

5. *Walla Walla Statesman,* October 4, 1882, p. 1.

6. *Walla Walla Statesman,* September 30, 1882, p. 3.

7. *Endicott Index,* August 16, 1935 and Henry Litzenberger interview, J.O. Oliphant file. The Henry Dayton Smiths were the first permanent settlers in the Endicott area. Smith filed a homestead and timber claim in 1878 on land just west of the future townsite and moved there from Walla Walla in the fall of 1879. Smith's wife, Jenny, was the daughter of Major and Mrs. R.H. Wimpy who had come west in a wagon train after the Civil War. The Smith home near Endicott became known as the Half-way House due to its location between Walla Walla and Spokane and they provided lodging and meals for freighters and other travelers. When the Oregon Improvement Company began surveying operations along Rebel Flat in July, 1880, the local agent, John Courtright, arranged for employee accomodations at the Half-way House. Jefferson T. Person also arrived in the summer of 1880 and later in the year opened the first store in the community.

8. *Endicott Index,* November 29, 1935, p. 1.

9. T.R. Tannatt, scrapbook clippings, 1878-83.

10. *Walla Walla Statesman,* October 21, 1882, p. 3.

11. Anna Weitz file.

12. Possibly by members of the Palouse bands who once owned huge herds along the lower Snake River but were defeated by Colonel George Wright in the Interior Indian Wars of 1855-58. In the 1880s they consisted of a few hundred individuals who were too proud to go to the reservation.

13. *Endicott Index,* December 6, 1935, p. 1.

14. Bryan, p. 163.

15. Letter, Tannatt to C.H. Prescott, Portland, Oregon, April 27, 1882.

16. *Endicott Index,* December 6, 1935, p. 1 and Anna Weitz file.

17. Henry J Winser, *Guide to the Northern Pacific Railroad and its Allied Lines* (New York: G.P. Putnam's Sons, 1883), pp. 219-20.

18. Jacob Adler, private interview, Tekoa, Washington, January 2, 1973.

19. Meinig, p. 272.

20. Dave Schierman, private interview, Walla Walla, Washington, July 9, 1972.

21. This being the northwest corner of Section 9, Township 17 N., Range 41 E.W.M., see *Whitman County Auditor Reports, 1885-1890.*

22. Anna Weitz file.

23. Dave Schierman interview.

24. C.G. Schmick, private interview, Colfax, Washington, April 14, 1969, and as related in Schlommer, pp. 61-62.

25. *Palouse Gazette,* April 24, 1885, p. 3.

26. Dave Schierman interview.

27. Gordon L. Lindeen, "Settlement and Development of Endicott, Washington to 1930" (Unpublished Master's Thesis, State College of Washington, 1960), p. 80.

28. Dave Schierman interview.

29. Meinig, pp. 406-07. The raising of Turkey Red, a hard red wheat, was introduced in America by Mennonites who emigrated from Russia to Kansas in the 1870s. It later revolutionized the Midwest grain industry.

30. Carrie Adell Strahorn, *Fifteen Thousand Miles by Stage* (New York, 1911), pp. 304-05.

31. *Ritzville Journal-Times,* "Adams County Pioneer Edition." September 15, 1949.

32. Roy Oestrich file, newspaper clipping quoting *The West Shore,* April, 1883.

33. Meinig, p. 339. For an extensive sociological study on the German Russians in the Ritzville area, see Elmer Miller, "The European Background and Assimilation of a Russian-German Group" (Unpublished Master's Thesis, State College of Washington, 1929).

34. Roy Oestreich file.

35. Winser, p. 219.

36. Jean Roth, "Walla Walla, Washington," *Unsere Leute Von Walter,* I (June, 1978), p. 15, and Mr. and Mrs. George Gradwohl, Jr., private interview, Walla Walla, Washington, March 18, 1978.

37. Sallet, p. 48.

38. Wanda Jane Schwabauer, "The Portland Community of Germans from Russia," unpublished typescript, May, 1974, pp. 18, 25, 33.

39. Sallet, pp. 48, 61.

40. Meinig, p. 277.

41. *Ibid.,* p. 372.

42. *Ibid.* For a detailed study of settlement in the Odessa area, see Oscar M. Undeberg, "Odessa, Washington: A History of its Settlement and Development to 1920" (Unpublished Master's Thesis, Washington State University, 1970).

43. Jacob Weber, private interview, Quincy, Washington, April 17, 1980.

44. Faye Morris, *They Claimed a Desert* (Fairfield, Washington: Ye Galleon Press, 1976), p. 46.

45. Sallet, p. 123.

46. Mr. and Mrs. Leo Lautenschlager, private interview, Brewster, Washington, April 17, 1980.

47. *S.S. Hungaria* Passenger List (to New York, May 15, 1888).

48. Mrs. Elizabeth Repp, private interview, Endicott, Washington, April 1, 1977.

49. Mr. and Mrs. Alfred Poffenroth, private interview, Calgary, Alberta, July 5, 1977.

50. *Mecca Glen Memories* (Ponoka, Alberta: Mecca Glen Centennial Committee, 1968), pp. 223-25, quoting Henry Scheuerman interview.

51. Mr. and Mrs. Walter Scheuerman, private interview, Bashaw, Alberta, July 1, 1977.

52. *Mecca Glen Memories,* pp. 222, 225.

53. *The Calgary Herald,* May 25, 1957, p. 7.

54. Jacob Meininger, Jacob Miller and Jacob Rehn, private interviews, Tacoma, Washington, April 4, 1978.

55. Dale Wirsing, *Builders, Brewers and Burghers: Germans of Washington State* (Washington State American Bicentennial Commission, 1977), p. 40.

56. Sallet, p. 31.

57. Among Volga German families in the Big Bend country, one finds the names Adler, Amen, Bauer, Bastrom, Becker, Benzel, Bitterman, Boos, Braun, Dewald, Eckhardt (Ekhart), Fink, Gettman, Gradwohl, Greenwalt, Hardt, Heimbigner, Hilzer, Hoffman, Homberg, Hopp, Horst, Ils, Kanzler, Kembel, Kiez, Kinzel, Kissler, Koch, Kramer, Krehn, Lesle, Lenhart, Maier, Melcher, Miller, Oestreich, Pfeiffer, Rehn, Rogel,

225

Rosenoff (Rosenauer), Rudy, Schauerman, Schoessler (Schessler), Schmidt, Starkel, Steinmetz, Stumpf, Thaut, Thiel, Wacker, Wagner, Walter, Weber, Wertemberger, Werzel, Wilhelm, Wolsborn, Zeller, and Zier.

58. Volga German family names in the Palouse country include Adler, Appel, Aschenbrenner, Bafus, Benner, Beutel, Blumenschein, Daubert, Dippel, Fisher, Geier, Gerlitz, Getz, Green, Helm, Hergert, Holstein, Kaiser, Kleweno (Klaveno), Koch (Cook), Konschu, Kromm, Langlitz, Lautenschlager (Lauten), Leinweber, Litzenberger, Luft, Lust, Machleit, Merkel, Moore, Morasch, Miller, Ochs, Poffenroth (Pfaff), Rausch, Reich, Repp, Ruhl, Schaeffer, Scheuerman (Schierman), Schukart, Stang, Wagner, Weitz, and Youngman.

59. Sallet, p. 123. German families from the Volga who settled in the Walla Walla area included those named Amen, Buterus, Daerr (Daire), Dietz, Fox, Frank, Fries, Gies, Gottwig, Gradwohl, Hamburg, Hill, Ills (Els), Mueller (Miller), Oswald, Reiter, Roth, Schmidt, Schneidmiller, Schoessler (Schlesser), Schreiner, Streck, Vols, Walter, and Zier.

60. Elaine Davidson, "Autobiography of Wilhelm (William) Frank," *Unsere Leute Von Kautz,* I (May, 1979), pp. 17-21 and Mr. and Mrs. William Schneidmiller, private interview, Walla Walla, Washington, April 13, 1980.

61. Art Eichler, private interview, Yakima, Washington, June 31, 1979.

62. Sallet, p. 112.

63. *Ibid.,* p. 123.

CHAPTER VI

1, Sallet, p. 112.

2. According to estimates for 1930, Evangelical Volga German membership nationally was as follows: Lutheran, 45%; Congregational, 30%; other Protestant denominations, 25%; See Koch, p. 120.

3. Eisenach, *A History of the German Congregational Churches....,* p. 131.

4. *Ibid.,* p. 46, quoting *The Home Missionary,* December, 1881, pp. 229 ff.

5. *Ibid.,* pp. 46-48.

6. *Ibid.,* p. 56. Two other German Congregational Churches were organized at Ritzville; Zion (1888) and Philadelphia (1912).

7. *Ibid.* The Walla Walla Congregation disbanded in 1884 but was reorganized in 1896.

8. Congregational work in Colfax was begun by the pioneer missionary of the Home Missionary Society, Rev. Cushing Eels, in the summer of 1874. The Plymouth congregation was organized there by him in July, 1877 following his move from Puget Sound where he had been active in Indian mission work. The Congregational Association of Washington Territory was formed in 1879 and a meeting on September 5th of that year in

Colfax established a regional district which became known as the Upper Columbia Conference. Active in Congregational mission work in the area during the 1880s were Rev. George H. Atkinson, who had entered service in the Oregon Country in 1848, Rev. Thomas W. Walters who continued Eel's work in Colfax in 1882 and Rev. Jonathan Edwards who in 1886 had accepted a call to the Spokane Falls congregation.

9. *Minutes of the Congregational Association of Oregon and Washington 1887,* Portland, 1887, p. 51.

10. Eisenach, *A History of the German Congregational Churches....,* p. 57. Rev. Gottfried Graedel, longtime Washington German Congregational Conference missionary, wrote that the Endicott council was led by Rev. Atkinson, Walters, and Edwards.

11. *Ibid.,* p. 290.

12. *Ibid.,* p. 136.

13. *Ibid.,* pp. 99-103. The following ministers and delegates represented the seven churches at the Portland Conference: 1) Portland Ebenezer; P. Yost, C. Yost, Mr. Krueger and Rev. J. Koch, 2) Beaverton Bethany; Mr. Graf, Mr. Siegenthaler and Rev. John Graef, 3) Endicott Evangelical Congregational; Rev. J. Hergert, 4) Seattle First German; Rev. J. Biegert, 5) Beaver Creek (Oregon) St. Peters; Mr. Grossmueller, Rev. R. Staub, 6) Ballard (Washington) German Congregational; Rev. G. Graedel, and 7) Stafford (Oregon) German Congregational; Mr. Wolf and Mr. Schatz. Also present were Superintendent Eversz, who was elected moderator, Rev. G.F. Graedel, elected scribe, and Rev. C.F. Class. The large number of churches in the Odessa area was due to both widespread rural settlement of Russians German and the fact that the churches were often organized according to regional origin in Russia as the Volga and Black Sea Germans established separate congregations in the town and surrounding countryside.

14. *Ibid.,* p. 161.

15. U. Clifford Nelson, *Lutheranism in North America, 1914-1970* (Minneapolis: Augsburg Publishing House, 1972), p. 3.

16. For a detailed history of the Joint Synod, see C.V. Sheatsley, *History of the Evangelical Lutheran Joint Synod of Ohio and Other States* (Columbus, Ohio: Lutheran Book Concern, 1919).

17. Theodore C. Moeller, "The Development of Lutheranism in the Pacific Northwest with Specific Reference to the Northwest District, The Lutheran Church - Missouri Synod, Part I," *Concordia Historical Institute Quarterly, XXVIII* (Summer, 1955), pp. 58-62.

18. *Ibid.,* p. 65.

19. *Ibid.,* p. 63.

20. Walter H. Hellman, Ed., *The Story of the Northwestern District of the American Lutheran Church* (Dubuque, Iowa: Wartburg Press, 1941), p. 10

21. *The Lutheran Standard,* May 28, 1887, p. 176.

22. Hellman, p. 10.

23. *Ibid.*

24. Revs. A. Krause, H. Rieke, G.F. Pauschert and P. Groschupf, *Denkschrift zum Silber-Jubiläum des Washington Distrikts der Ev. Luth. Ohio Synode, 1891-1916* (Columbus, Ohio: Lutheran Book Concern, 1916), p. 74, hereafter cited as *DWD*.

25. *Ls,* February 28, 1891, p. 75.

26. *LS,* May 28, 1887, p. 176.

27. Rev. John Groschupf and others, *A Brief History of the Emmanuel Lutheran Church,* Spokane, Washington, 1939, p. 5.

28. *Verhandlungen des Washington Distrikts* (Columbus, Ohio: Lutheran Book Concern, 1914), p. 72. At the Archives of the American Lutheran Church, Dubuque, Iowa.

29. *Ibid.,* undated, p. 33.

30. *LS,* May 21, 1892, p. 21. This summary is in reference to the work of Pastors Mollenauer and Schneider in the Big Bend area.

31. Hellman, p. 10.

32. Moeller, p. 66.

33. Rev. H.J. Gieseke and others. *A Brief History of Zion Lutheran Church (Missouri Synod) at Endicott, Washington,* 1941, p. 3.

34. Moeller, p. 66.

35. Rev. R.H. Eckhoff and others, *Seventy-five Blessed Years, 1890-1965* (Zion Lutheran Church Anniversary Booklet), Tacoma, Washington, 1965, p. 3.

36. *LS,* August 5, 1893, p. 243.

37. *LS,* June 14, 1890, p. 1708.

38. *DWD,* pp. 66-70.

39. *Ibid.*

40. *LS,* June 7, 1890, p. 178. The school mentioned is probably a reference to the parochial school opened by Rev. Wolf at Trinity Lutheran Church in Tacoma during the summer of 1889. Professor Henry L. Wittrock, who had emigrated from Germany to Detroit, Michigan, accepted a call to become the first teacher at the Tacoma school and built it into a highly respected academy. See Hellman, p. 30, for a discussion of Wittrock's work and the history of the institution.

41. *LS,* June 14, 1890, p. 1708.

42. Schuh's vehement response to this can be seen in his report published in the *Lutheran Standard,* December 12, 1891, p. 395. Earlier that year he had written, "Here is an opportunity to cast bread upon the waters and after many days it shall return. There is so much to do that it is fairly confusing. The only discouraging feature in this work is the great cry of the people for pastors and our inability to serve them. May the Lord of the harvest send us help out of Zion!" *LS,* February 28, 1891, p. 75.

43. *LS,* June 14, 1891, p. 1708.

44. *DWD,* p. 82.

45. Letter, Rieke to Groschupf, May 5, 1890.

46. *Ibid.*

47. Hellman, pp. 10-11.

48. *Ibid.,* p. 9.

49. *DWD,* pp. 3-4. The pioneers present who effectuated the organization of the district at the Tacoma conclave, in the order in which they entered service in the Far West, were: Pastors F.N. Wolf, Tacoma; A.H. Horn, The Dalles; H.H. Rieke, Genesee; P.F. Hein, Spokane; C. Lembke, Lake Bay,; A. Krause, Tacoma; L.H. Schuh, Tacoma; P. Groschupf, Genesee; C.F. Vollmer, Walla Walla; E. Hasse, Leber; J. Willers, Tacoma and Teacher H.L. Wittrock, Tacoma. Pastor C. Pitzler from Fairfield was formally excused due to his inability to attend. District officers elected for the first synodical year were: Pastors L.H. Schuh, president; P.F. Hein, vice-president; A. Krause, secretary; C.F. Vollmer, treasurer; and P. Groschupf, chaplain.

50. *Verhandlungen der ersten Versammlung des Washington - Distrikts der Allgem. Ev. Luth. Synode von Ohio u. a. St.* (Columbus, Ohio, 1891), pp. 8-10.

51. *LS,* December 9, 1891, p. 402.

52. *LS,* November 19, 1892, p. 373 and *LS,* April 16, 1892, p. 131. At this time, when immigration to Eastern Washington was rapidly peopling the land, the Mission fields labored in by many of these Lutheran pastors were still great. The following listing demonstrates the extent of their work in 1892 (dates indicate the years the churches were constituted):

Rev. P.H. Hein: Spokane (Emmanuel, 1889).

Rev. H. Rieke: Fairfield (Zion, 1890), Farmington (Christ Lutheran, 1896) and Spangle.

Rev. P. Groschupf: Cameron (Emmanuel, 1888), Genesee (St. John's, 1888), Uniontown, Palouse and Moscow (Emmanuel, 1902). Together with Rev. Rieke: Endicott (Trinity, 1890) and Colfax (Peace, 1902.

Rev. W.H. Kropp: Sprague (St. John's, 1891), Lind (Good Hope, 1903) and Ritzville (Emmanuel, 1891).

Rev. L. H. Mollenauer: Readan (Emmanuel, 1891). Davenport (Zion, 1891), Egypt (Christ Church, 1891), Almira and Wilbur (St. Paul's 1900).

Rev. A.F. Gillman: Walla Walla (Emmanuel, reorganized 1890). Sixteen families withdrew from Walla Walla's Emmanuel Lutheran Church in 1896 to establish a more centrally located congregation which became Christ Lutheran Church. One pastor served both congregations until the growth of the Christ Lutheran, largely due to the influx of Volga Germans, enabled them to call Rev. C. Wellsandt as their first permanent pastor in 1912. See Rev. Foege and others, *Emmanuel Lutheran Church 75th Anniversary,* Walla Walla, 1963 and *DWD,* pp. 82-84.

53. Moeller, p. 67. Rev. Theiss had also organized St. Paul's Lutheran Church in Portland in 1889 but a debate arose over the possible relocation of the church and the synod's into the Ohio Synod, calling Rev. C.F.W. All-

wardt as their new pastor. *See DWD*, p. 54.

54. *Ibid.*, p. 58.

55. Gieseke and others, p. 3.

56. *Oregon - Washington Distrikt, Synodal-Bericht*, 1901. (Translated by K. Lorenz, St. Louis: Concordia Publishing House, 1901, p. 5).

57. Moeller, p. 76.

58. *Ibid.*, p. 77.

59. Gieseke and others, p. 3.

60. Doering journal entries forwarded with letter to Mission Board, 1902, as quoted in Moeller, pp. 74-75.

61. *Ibid.*

62. *DWD*, p. 22.

63. *Ibid.*, p. 26.

64. U.S. Bureau of Census, *Religious Bodies, 1916*, Part I, *Abstract*, 1919, p. 324.

65. *Ibid.*, p. 323.

66. Hellman, p. 23.

67. Riasanovsky, pp. 540-41.

68. Emma D. Schwabenland, *A History of the Volga Relief Society* (Portland, Oregon: A.E. Kern & Co., 1941), p. 127, hereafter cited as *VRS*. Hoover's American Relief Administration distributed $61,500,000 worth of food, clothing and medicine in Russia in response to the Soviet's appeal for aid during the famine. The Volga Relief Society was one of many groups that raised funds for the starving populace in Russia at this time as Quaker, Catholic and Mennonite organizations also joined the effort.

69. Bonwetsch, p. 122 and *VRS*, p. 30.

70. 1 pood = 36 pounds.

71. Letter in the possession of the author, translated by Karl Scheuerman.

72. Mr. and Mrs. George Repp file, quoted in *VRS*, p. 33.

73. *VRS*, p. 34. Officers elected at the Portland meeting included John W. Miller, president; David Hilderman, vice-president; George Repp, secretary and John H. Krieger, treasurer (replaced by Gottfried Geist a week later).

74. *Ibid.*, pp. 34-35.

75. *Ibid.*, pp. 36-39. The following excerpt is from the Volga Relief Society's financial statement of contributions as of December, 1922 (see *VRS*, p. 82):

Oregon

Portland	$29,576.86
Salem	15.00
Ruckles	15.00

WASHINGTON

Odessa	4,184.83
Walla Walla	2,456.95
Ritzville	2,384.00
Endicott	1,415.50
Dryden	1,203.51
Waterville	930.00
Tacoma	597.50
Quincy	418.60
Alkali Flats	315.00
Warden	206.75
Ralston	154.50
Seattle	120.55
Wapato	50.00
Snoqualmie	50.00
Sunnyside	20.00
Blaine	15.00
Wilkinson	12.50

76. *VRS*, p. 69.

77. Mr. and Mrs. George Repp file, quoted in *VRS*, p. 93.

78. *Ibid.*, pp. 91-92.

79. *Ibid.*, pp. 87-88.

80. Sallet, p. 105.

81. Mr. and Mrs. George Repp file, quoted in *VRS*, p. 122.

BIBLIOGRAPHY
BOOKS AND PAMPHLETS

Bauer, Gottlieb. *Geschichte der Deutschen in den Wolgakolonien*. Saratov, 1907.

Beratz, Gottlieb. *Die deutschen Kolonien an der Unteren Wolga*. Saratov: H. Schellhorn u. Co., 1915; sd ed., Berline: Verband der wolgadeutschen Bauern, G.m.b.H. 1923.

Bonwetsch, Gerhard. *Geschichte der deutschen Kolonien an der Wolga*. Stuttgart: Verlag von J. Englehorns Nachf. 1919.

Bryan, Enoch A. *Orient Meets Occident: The Advent of the Railways to the Pacific Northwest*. Pullman, Washington: The Students Book Corporation, 1936.

Burgdorff H. George. *Erlebnisse als Missionar oder Reiseprediger in Russland*. Hillsboro, Kansas: M.B. Publishing House, 1924.

Collard, Rev. Ernest and others. *Peace Lutheran Church Fiftieth Anniversary, 1909-1959*. Tacoma, Washington. 1959.

Duin, Edgar C. *Lutheranism under the Tsars and Soviets*. 2 vols. Ann Arbor, Michigan: University Microfilms. 1975.

Durant, Will. *The Reformation: A History of European Civilization from Wyclif to Calvin, 1300-1564*. New York: Simon and Schuster. 1957.

Eisenach, George J. *A History of the German Congregational Churches in the United States*. Yankton, South Dakota: The Pioneer Press. 1938.

_____. *Pietism and the Russian Germans*. Berne, Indiana: The Berne Publishers. 1949.

_____. *Das religiöse Leben unter den Russlanddeutschen in Russland und Amerika*. Marburg an der Lahn, W. Ger.: Buchdruckerei Hermann Rathmann. 1950

Eckhoff, Rev. R.H. and others. *Seventy-five Blessed Years, 1890-1965*. Zion Lutheran Church Anniversary Booklet. Tacoma, Washington. 1965.

E(rbes), J. and P. S(inner). *Volkslieder und Kinderreime aus den Wolgakolonien*. Saratov: Buchdruckerei Energie. 1914.

Fairchild, Henry Pratt. *Immigration*. New York: John Wiley and Sons, Inc. 1925.

Foege, Rev. W. and others. *Emmanuel Lutheran Church 75th Anniversary*. Walla Walla. 1963.

Forty-fifth Annual Reunion of the Association of the Graduates of the United States Military Academy. Saginaw, Michigan: Seemans and Peters, Inc. 1914.

Gieseke, Rev. H.J. and others. *A Brief History of Zion Lutheran Church (Missouri Synod) at Endicott, Washington*. 1941.

232

Giesenger, Adam. *From Catherine to Krushchev.* Battleford, Saskatchewan: Marian Press. 1974.

Groschupf, Rev. John and others. *The Story of Fifty Years: A Brief History of the Emmanuel Lutheran Church, 1889-1939.* Spokane, Washington. 1939.

Hansen, Marcus Lee. *The Immigrant in American History.* Cambridge: Harvard University Press. 1940.

Haxthausen, August von. *Studien über die inneren Zustaende des Volkslebens und insebsondere der laendlichen Einrichtungen Russlands.* Hanover, 1847-1852. (Translated by Eleanore L. M. Schmidt: *Studies on the Interior of Russia.* Chicago: University of Chicago Press. 1972.)

Hedges, James Blain. *Henry Villard and the Railways of the Northwest.* New Haven: Yale University Press. 1930.

Height, Joseph S. *Paradise on the Steppe.* Bismark, N.D.: North Dakota Historical Society of Germans from Russia. 1972.

Hellman, Walter H., Ed. *Fifty Golden Years: The Story of the Northwest District of the American Lutheran Church, 1891-1941.* Dubuque, Iowa: Wartburg Press. 1941.

Klaus Aleksandr Avgustovich. *Nashii kolonii: Opyty materialy po istorii i statistike inostrannoi kolonizatsii v rossi.* St. Petersburg: Tipografiia V.V. Nusval't. 1869.

Koch, Fred C. *The Volga Germans: In Russia and the Americas, From 1763 to the Present.* University Park: Pennsylvania State University Press. 1977.

Krause, Revs. A., H. Rieke, G. F. Pauschert and P. Groschupf. *Denkschrift zum Silber-Jubiläum des Washington Distrikts der Ev. Luth. Ohio Synode, 1891-1916.* Columbus, Ohio: Lutheran Book Concern. 1916.

Lavender, David. *Land of Giants: The Drive to the Pacific Northwest, 1750-1950.* Garden City, New York: Doubleday and Co., 1958.

Luebke, Frederick C. *Immigrants and Politics: The Germans of Nebraska, 1880-1900.* Lincoln: University of Nebraska Press. 1969.

Mecca Glen Memories. Ponoka, Alberta: Mecca Glen Centennial Committee. 1968.

Meinig, Donald W. *The Great Columbia Plain: A Historical Geography, 1805-1910.* Seattle: University of Washington Press. 1968.

Morris, Faye. *They Claimed A Desert.* Fairfield, Washington: Ye Galleon Press. 1976.

Nelson, E. Clifford. *Lutheranism in North America, 1914-1970.* Minneapolis: Augsburg Publishing House. 1972.

Ochs, Grace Lillian. *Up From the Volga: The Story of the Ochs Family.* Nashville: Southern Publishing Association. 1969.

Pallas, Peter Simon. *Reisen durch verschiedene Provinzen des russischen Reiches in den Jahren 1768-1774.* St. Petersburg, 1771-1776.

Pissarevskii, Grigorii G. *Iz istorii inostrannoi kolonizatsii v rossii v XVIII v. (Po neizdannym arkhivnym dokumentam.)* Moskva: A.I. Snegirevyi. 1909.

——. *Vnutrennii rasporiadok v koloniiakh povolzh'ia pri Ekaterine II.* Varshava: Tipografiliia varshavskago uchebnago okruga. 1914.

Protokoll der im Jahr 1889 zu Saratov abgehaltenen 16-ten combinirten Synode der bei den Wolga-Präposituren. Saratov: Prapositur der Wolga. 1889.

Raugust, W.C., R. Hoefel, Rev. A. Rehn and Rev. A. Hausauer. *History of the Pacific Conference of Congregational Churches of Washington, Oregon and Idaho, 1897-1964.* 1964.

Riasanovsky, Nicholas V. *A History of Russia (Second Edition).* New York: Oxford University Press. 1969.

Sallet, Richard. *Russian-German Settlements in the United States.* Fargo: North Dakota Institute for Regional Studies. 1974. Translated by LaVern J. Rippley and Armand Bauer.

Schleuning, Johannes. *Die deutschen Kolonien im Wolgagebiet.* Berlin, 1919. Reprint. Portland, Ore.: A.E. Kern & Co., 1922.

Schmidt, David. *Studien uber die Geschichte der Wolgadeutschen.* Pokrowsk, A.S.S.R. der Wolgadeutschen: Zentral-Völker-Verlag. 1930.

Schnaible, Rev. Fred and others. *A History of Trinity Lutheran Church, 1887-1975.* Dedication Anniversary Booklet. Endicott, Washington. 1975.

Schul - und Küster-Schülmeister Instruction in den evangelischen Kolonien des Saratovschen und Samaraschen Gouvernments. Moscow: Evangelisch-Lutherischen Consistorio. Undated.

Schwabenland, Emma D. *A History of the Volga Relief Society.* Portland: A.B. Kern & Co. 1941.

Sheatsley, C.V. *History of the Evangelical Lutheran Joint Synod of Ohio and Other States.* Columbus, Ohio: Lutheran Book Concern. 1919.

Snowden, Clinton. *A History of Washington: The Rise and Progress of an American State.* 6 Vols. New York: The Century History Company. 1909

Strahorn, Carrie A. *Fifteen Thousand Miles by Stage.* New York. 1911.

Stumpp, Karl. *The Emigration from Germany to Russia in the Years 1763 to 1862.* Tübingen, Germany: by the author. 1973.

——. *The German-Russians: Two Centuries of Pioneering.* Trostberg, Germany: A. Erdl. 1967. (Translated by Dr. Joseph Height).

Thomson, Gladys Scott. *Catherine the Great and the Expansion of Russia.* New York: Collier Books. 1965.

Villard, Henry. *The Early History of Transportation in Oregon.* Eugene: University of Oregon Press. 1944.

Volz, Jacob. *Historical Review of the Balzerer.* York, Nebraska. 1938.

Wagner, Rev. Albert F. and others. *Emmanuel Lutheran Church Diamond Anniversary.* Ritzville, Washington. 1965.

Weitz, Anna. *History of the Evangelical Congregational Church, 1883-1963.* Endicott, Washington. 1963.

Williams, Hattie Plum. *The Czars Germans: With Particular Reference to the Volga Germans.* Lincoln, Nebraska: The American Historical Society of Germans from Russia. 1975.

Winsor, Henry J. *The Great Northwest: A Guidebook and Itinerary for the use of Tourists and Travellers Over the lines of the Northern Pacific Railroad.* New York: G.P. Putnam's Sons. 1883.

Wirsing, Dale R. *Builders, Brewers and Burghers: Germans of Washington State.* The Washington State American Revolution Bicentennial Commission. 1977.

Yungman, Susan M. *Faith of our Fathers.* By the author. 1972.

Zorrow, William F. *Kansas: A History of the Jayhawk State.* Norman: University of Oklahoma Press. 1957.

Züge, Christian Gottlob. *Der russiche Kolonist.* I. Zeitz und Naumberg: Wilhelm Webel. 1802.

PERIODICALS AND OFFICIAL MINUTES

Davidson, Elaine, Ed. "Autobiography of Wilhelm (William) Frank," *Unsere Leute Von Kautz,* I (May, 1979), 17-21.

Dudek, Pauline B. "Further Notes on the Wagon Train from Nebraska to Washington," *AHSGR Journal,* II, No. 3 (Winter, 1979), 44-46.

Esselborn, Karl. "Die Auswanderung von Hessen nach Russland," *Heimat im Bild,* 1926, 83-104.

Flegel, Art and Cleora. "Research in Hesse," *AHSGR Work Paper* No. 13 (December, 1973), 21-27.

Haynes, Emma S. "Germans from Russia in American History and Literature," *AHSGR Work Paper* No. 15 (September, 1974), 4-20.

. "Researching in the National Archives," *AHSGR Journal,* II, No. 1 (Spring, 1979), 4-7.

Hoezler, Johann. "The Earliest Volga Germans in Sutton, Nebraska and a Portion of their History," *AHSGR Work Paper* No. 16 (December, 1974), 16-18. (Translated by Art Flegel).

Kloberdanz, Timothy. "Funery Beliefs and Customs of the Germans from Russia," *AHSGR Work Paper* No. 20 (Spring, 1976), 15-20.

Kromm, Georg. "Die deutschen Ansiedler an der Wolga," *Schottener Kreisblatt,* Redaktion, Druck und Verlag von Wilhelm Engel, Schotten, Germany, Nos. 15-17, 21 (February, March, 1910).

Moeller, Theodore C., Jr. "The Development of Lutheranism in the Pacific Northwest with Specific Reference to the Northwest District, the Lutheran Church-Missouri Synod, Part I," *Concordia Historical Institute Quarterly,* XXVIII (Summer, 1955), 49-86.

Oregon-Washington Distrikt, Synode-Bericht, 1901 (Missouri Synod). Translated by K. Lorenz, 1901. At the District Archives, Portland, Oregon.

Rempel, David G. "The Mennonite Commonwealth in Russia: A Sketch of its Founding and Endurance, 1789-1919," *Mennonite Quarterly Review,* XLVII (October, 1973) and XLVIII (January, 1974)

Roth, Jean, "Walla Walla, Washington," *Unsere Leute Von Walter,* I (June, 1978), 15.

Saul, Norman E. "The Arrival of the Germans from Russia: A Centennial Perspective," *AHSGR Work Paper* No. 21 (Fall, 1976), 4-11.

. "The Migration of Russian-Germans to Kansas," *Kansas Historical Quarterly,* XL, No. 1 (Spring, 1974), 38-62.

Schlommer, Harm. "Inland Empire Russia Germans," *The Pacific Northwesterner,* VIII (Fall, 1964), 57-64.

Stärkel, Johannes. "Johann Wilhelm Stärkel aus Norka unter der Fahne Pugachews," *Friedensbote* (November, 1901), 685-688.

Stumpp, Karl. "Verzeichnis der ev. Pastoren in den deutschen und gemischtenvor allem in Städten-Kirchenspielen in Russland bzw. der Sowjetunion, ohne Baltikum und Polen," *Heimatbuch der Deutschen aus Russland,* 1972, 276-389.

Verhandlungen des Washington Distrikts (Ohio Synod), 1891-24, Columbus, Ohio. At the Archives of the American Lutheran Church, Dubuque, Iowa.

Wagner, Ernst. "Auswanderung aus Hessen," *Auslanddeutschtum und evangelischen Kirche Jahrbuch,* 1938, 24-33.

Würz, Wilhelm "Wie Jagodnaja Poljana gegrundet wurde," *Heimatbuch der Deutschen aus Russland,* 1962, 65-66.

MANUSCRIPT MATERIALS

Frank, John W. "A Brief History of the Russian-Germans in the Evangelical and Reformed Church." Unpublished Bachelor of Divinity Thesis, Eden Theological Seminary, Webster Grove, Missouri. 1945.

Lindeen, Gordon L. "Settlement and Development of Endicott, Washington to 1930." Unpublished Master's Thesis, Washington State University. 1960.

Miller, Elmer. "The European Background and Assimilation of a Russian-German Group." Unpublished Master's Thesis, State College of Washington. 1960.

Scholz, Harry G. "The German Colonists of Russia: The Repeal of Russia's Law of the Colonists in 1871 and its effect on the German Colonist Population." Unpublished Master's Thesis, Chapman College, Orange, California. 1929.

Schwabauer, Wanda J. "The Portland Community of Germans from Russia." Xeroxed Typescript. 1974.

Schwabenland, Emma D. "German-Russians on the Volga and in the United States." Unpublished Master's Thesis, University of Colorado, Boulder, Colorado. 1929.

Scheuerman, Richard D. "Patterns of Settlement in the Palouse Country, 1860-1915." Unpublished Manuscript. 1980

Swanson, Robert W. "A History of Logging and Lumbering on the Palouse River, 1870-1905." Unpublished Master's Thesis, State College of Washington. 1958.

Thiel, Ruth, "Memories of my Father." Mimeographed Typescript. Undated.

Undeberg, Oscar M. "Odessa, Washington: A History of its Settlement and Development to 1920." Unpublished Master's Thesis, Washington State University. 1970

Vogt, Don. "Whitman County, Washington Germans from Russia." Unpublished Manuscript. 1980.

NEWS ARTICLES

Calgary Herald. Calgary, Alberta. May 25, 1957.

Endicott Index. Endicott, Washington. 1919, 1928, 1935-36.

Hays City Sentinel. Hays City, Kansas. August 16, 1876.

London Times. London, England. February 1, 1876.

Lutheran Standard. Columbus, Ohio. 1887-95.

Palouse Gazette. Colfax, Washington. 1882-85.

Ritzville Journal-Times. "Adams County Pioneer Edition," September 15, 1949. 1950.

Russel Record. Russel, Kansas. December 7, 1876.

Topeka Daily Blade. Topeka, Kansas. December 13, 1875.

Walla Walla Weekly Statesman. Walla Walla, Washington. 1882.

PUBLIC DOCUMENTS AND PAPERS

Church Anniversary Bulletins of the American Lutheran Church. At the North Pacific District Archives, Seattle, Washington.

Hesse, *Acten des Geheimen Staats-Archives, XI,* Abhteilung, Convolut I. At the Hessen State Archives, Darmstadt, West Germany.

Kromm, Georg, Ed. *Einwanderliste von Jagodnaja Poljana (aus Hessen).* At the Vogelsberg Museum in Schotten, West Germany.

Russia, *Polnoe Sobranie Zakonov Rossiiskoi Imperii. Sankt Peterburg, 1649-1916.* At the Hoover Library and Institute, Stanford University, Stanford, California.

Oliphant, J. Orin. Unpublished papers. At the Holland Library Archives, Washington State University, Pullman, Washington.

Oregon Improvement Company. *Annual Business Reports, 1881-1890.* At the Suzallo Library, Special Collections, University of Washington, Seattle, Washington.

Oregon Improvement Company Letter File. At the Holland Library Archives, Washington State University, Pullman, Washington.

Tannatt, Thomas R. Private letter file and scrapbook clippings, 1878-1883. At the Holland Library Archives, Washington State University, Pullman, Washington.

U.S. Bureau of the Census. *Thirteenth Census of the United States: 1910. Abstract,* 1912.

U.S. Bureau of the Census. *Religious Bodies: 1916,* Part I. *Abstract,* 1919.

U.S. National Archives. *Manifests of Vessels arriving at New York, 1820-1897. S.S. Ohio* (to Baltimore) (November 23, 1875), *S.S. City of Chester* (July 10, 1876), *S.S. Donau* (August 5, 1876), *S.S. Mosel* (October 24, 1876), *S.S. Frisia* (December 8, 1876), *S.S. Hungaria* (May 15, 1888), *S.S. Wieland* (June 5, 1878), *S.S. City of Montreal* (January 6, 1876).

Washington Territorial Census. *Whitman County, 1883* (Microfilm copy). At the Holland Library Archives. Washington State University, Pullman, Washington.

Weitz, Anna B. Unpublished papers. At the Holland Library Archives, Washington State University, Pullman, Washington.

Whitman County *Auditor Reports, 1885-1892.* At the Whitman County Courthouse, Colfax, Washington.

ORAL INTERVIEWS

Adler, Jacob. Tekoa, Washington, January 2, 1973.

Bafus, Mrs. John. Endicott, Washington, April 29, 1980.

Blumenschein, Mr. Conrad. St. John, Washington, May 6 and 13, 1980.

Engelland, Hazel (Tannatt). Lacey, Washington, April 20, 1978.

Eichler, Art. Yakima, Washington, June 31, 1979.

Gradwohl, Mr. & Mrs. George, Jr. Walla Walla, Washington, March 18, 1978.

Greenwalt, Mr. & Mrs. John. Quincy, Washington, April 2, 1976.

Koch, Peter. Portland, Oregon, June 15, 1977.

Kromm, Elizabeth. Lacrosse, Washington, June 10, 1979.

Lautenschlager, Mr. & Mrs. Leo. Brewster, Washington, April 17, 1980.

Litzenberger, Henry. Deer Park, Washington, May 4, 1980.

Luft, Catherine. Sheboygan, Wisconsin, June 15-19, 1977.

Lust, Martin. Colfax, Washington, April 7, 1975.

Markel, August. Endicott, Washington, June 19, 1970.

Meininger, Jacob. Tacoma, Washington, April 4, 1978.

Miller, Jacob. Tacoma, Washington, April 4, 1978.

Morasch, Mrs. A.P. Endicott, Washington, March 4, 1980.

Morasch, Mrs. C.P. Endicott, Washington, April 23, 1971.

Ochs, Ed. Cashmere, Washington, March 17, 1977.

Ochs, Mr. & Mrs. Dan. St. Helena, California, February 16, 1974.

Ochs, Leta, Endicott, Washington, April 23, 1971.

Oestreich, Mr. & Mrs. Roy. Ritzville, Washington, April 1, 1978.

Poffenroth, Mr. & Mrs. Alfred. Calgary, Alberta, July 5, 1977.

Rehn, Jacob, Tacoma, Washington, April 4, 1978.

Reich, Alec. Endicott, Washington, April 2, 1969.

Repp, Elizabeth. Endicott, Washington, April 1, 1971.

Rieke, Mr. & Mrs. H.H. Cashmere, Washington, October 10, 1975.

Scheuerman, Karl. Endicott, Washington, December 10, 1969.

Scheuerman, Una Mae. Endicott, Washington, June 8, 1975.

Scheuerman, Mr. & Mrs. Walter. Bashaw, Alberta, July 1, 1977.

Schierman, Dave. Walla Walla, Washington, July 9, 1972.

Schierman, Mr. & Mrs. John. Vulcan, Alberta, July 2, 1977.

Schmick, Conrad G. Colfax, Washington, April 14, 1969.

Schneidmiller, Mr. & Mrs. William. Walla Walla, Washington, April 13, 1980.

Weber, Jacob. Quincy, Washington, April 17. 1980.

PRIVATE FILES AND CORRESPONDENCE

Dudek, Pauline. Letter to the author. Bladen, Nebraska, March 1, 1978.

Hausauer, Rev. Albert. Unpublished papers. Odessa, Washington.

Haynes, Emma S. Letter to the author. Arlington, Virginia, November 19, 1977.

Horst, Alec. Unpublished papers. Tacoma, Washington.

Miller, Earl. Unpublished papers. Endicott, Washington.

Ochs, Leta. Scrapbook clippings. Endicott, Washington.

Oestreich, Roy. Unpublished papers. Ritzville, Washington.

Reich, Evelyn. Unpublished papers. Colfax, Washington.

Roth, Jean. Unpublished papers. Seattle, Washington.

Scheirman, William. Letter to the author. Overland Park, Kansas, February 10, 1977.

Scheuerman, Richard D. Unpublished letters from Russia, 1920-1940. Endicott, Washington.

Scott, Betty. Unpublished papers. Mission, Kansas.

Wilhelm, Laurin P. Letter to the author. Lawrence, Kansas, April 27, 1974

INDEX

242

244

245